British Population in the Twentieth Century

N. L. Tranter

D0243050

First published 1996 by
MACMILLAN PRESS LTD
Houndmills, Basingstoke, Hampshire RG21 6XS
and London
Companies and representatives
throughout the world

500056372

ISBN 0–333–59762–1 hardcover
ISBN 0–333–59763–X paperback

A catalogue record for this book is available
from the British Library.

10   9   8   7   6   5   4   3   2   1
05   04   03   02   01   00   99   98   97   96

Printed in Malaysia

Published in the United States of America 1996 by
ST. MARTIN'S PRESS, INC.,
Scholarly and Reference Division
175 Fifth Avenue, New York, N.Y. 10010

ISBN 0–312–12940–8

TO HEATHER, RACHEL, SARAH AND ALAN

CONTENTS

TABLES

Tables

Map 1   Britain. Counties, planning regions and major towns, 1981

Source: Edward Royle, *Modern Britain. A Social History 1750–1985* (London, Edward Arnold, 1987), p. xii

Map 2 Scotland. Civil counties and regions, 1861–1939
Source: Michael Flinn (ed.), *Scottish Population History from the Seventeenth Century to the 1930s* (Cambridge, Cambridge University Press, 1977), p. xxiii

INTRODUCTION

At the beginning of the twentieth century the demography of each of the countries of mainland Britain was already an intriguing blend of the old and the new. In common with the experience of the preceding hundred years or so rates of population growth remained relatively high. A substantial proportion of each country's natural excess of births over deaths continued to disappear to overseas destinations. Changes in the internal geography of residence continued to favour England at the expense of Scotland and Wales, northern rather than southern counties of England, urban rather than rural locations, and core rather than more peripheral areas. Average expectations of life and variations in rates of mortality and life expectancy by region and socio-occupational class differed only moderately from those of a century earlier. Ages at marriage and percentages married and single had remained roughly constant for over 50 years. Crude birth rates were still only marginally lower than in the early nineteenth century and regional differentials in fertility were wider than ever. In these and many other respects the demographic structure of Britain around 1900 was little different from that of 1850 or even 1800.

At the same time, even before 1900, some of the demographic forms inherited from the past were beginning to change. In the course of the later decades of the nineteenth century the shift of population from south to north, rural to urban, and periphery to core started to slow. Regional, urban-rural and social class differentials in mortality began to narrow and average expectations of life to rise. Crude birth rates and levels of marital fertility began to decline and marital fertility replaced nuptiality as the principal demographic determinant of trends in overall fertility.

Compared with what was to happen in the twentieth century, it must be stressed, the changes which occurred in Britain's demographic structures in the decades before 1900 were modest. The late nineteenth century may have been the period in which the transition towards a modern demographic regime was initiated. But it was in the twentieth century that the bulk of the transformation was achieved.

Between 1800–9 and 1891–1900 average life expectancy at birth in England rose by about 11 years. Between 1891–1900 and the mid 1980s, chiefly in response to a decline in deaths from infectious disease and the displacement of communicable, infectious disease by non-communicable, degenerative disease as the main cause of death, it rose by over 26 years. In the half century before 1900 crude birth rates fell by just 15 per cent in England and Wales and 5 per cent in Scotland. In the course of the next 50 years they declined by 45 per cent and 39 per cent respectively. From around five among women marrying in the mid 1870s, the average number of births fell to around two among those marrying in the last quarter of the twentieth century. Accompanying this decline in fertility were marked reductions in regional and socio-occupational class fertility differentials and, in the later years of the century, unprecedented increases in the frequency of divorce, levels of extramarital cohabitation and rates of illegitimacy.

No less striking have been the changes that have taken place in patterns of migration and population growth. Between the 1930s and 1980s England and Wales together (though not Scotland), in sharp contrast to the experience of previous ages, gained far more people than they lost on balance of international migration. Despite this, rates of population

growth fell to levels lower than at any time since the late eighteenth century. By the 1970s and 1980s, under the impact of
persistently low levels of fertility, rates of population growth
were negligible and even negative. The trend to lower rates of
population increase was accompanied by major changes in the
geography of residence within Britain. Although England has
continued to increase its share of Britain's population and
although, within England, the ranking of regions according to
their share of the total population has remained largely unaltered, in contrast to what had happened in the nineteenth
century the twentieth century has seen the re-emergence of a
north to south drift in the balance of population location, a
movement of people from core to geographically more
peripheral regions, and a shift of people away from the largest
urban communities towards smaller urban communities and
rural areas.

In the demography of Britain at the beginning of the twentieth century there was still a great deal that generations born a
hundred years or more earlier would have recognised. In the
demography of Britain at the end of the twentieth century
there is very little that would be familiar to them. What follows
is an attempt to chart in more detail the progress of this transformation and to unravel some of the more important causes
which underlay it.

1

POPULATION GROWTH AND LOCATION

One of the most striking characteristics of British population history in the decades since the end of the First World War has been the persistence of rates of population increase far below those achieved in the century or so prior to 1914. As Table 1.2 shows, at their peak during the early decades of the nineteenth century rates of population growth in mainland Britain as a whole averaged from 1.4 per cent to 1.8 per cent a year. Between the 1840s and the first decade of the twentieth century they slowed, to between 1 per cent and 1.4 per cent. But it was not until the decade 1911–20 that the decline became pronounced. From the 1910s to the 1960s annual rates of population growth slumped to around 0.5 per cent. In the course of the following twenty years they declined still further. By the 1970s growth rates were negligible and by the 1980s even the absolute size of the population had begun to decline.

Broadly the chronology of population growth in each of the mainland countries followed much the same pattern. In England growth rates peaked during the early decades of the nineteenth century before settling at slightly lower levels in the period between the middle of the century and the outbreak of the First World War. With occasional exceptions in the late sixteenth and late eighteenth centuries, at no time since at least the mid sixteenth century have rates of English population growth approached those recorded between 1801 and 1911.[1] Between 1911 and 1920 they suddenly fell to less than 0.5 per cent a year, at which level they remained for the following five decades. In the 1970s there was a further sharp fall. By the 1980s, for the first time since the years of demographic crisis in the late seventeenth and early eighteenth centuries, even the absolute size of England's population declined.

In Wales and Scotland too rates of population increase peaked in the early nineteenth century before stabilising at lower, though still historically high, levels between the mid nineteenth century and the First World War. In the century before 1914 the pace of population growth in Wales was only marginally below that in England and in several decades, notably 1901–11, even exceeded it. The postwar decline in rates of population increase, however, was greater in Wales than in England. In every decade from the 1920s to the 1960s the population of Wales grew more slowly than that of England and in the 1920s and 1930s it actually decreased. During the 1970s and 1980s, on the other hand, rates of population growth in Wales exceeded those in England. Of all mainland countries only Wales avoided an absolute decline in population in the 1980s and only in Wales did the pace of population increase in the 1970s and 1980s not fall below the levels recorded in any other decade since the beginning of the nineteenth century.

Rates of population growth in Scotland during the nineteenth century were consistently lower than in either England or Wales. Except in the 1920s and 1930s, when they compared favourably with the Welsh experience, they have remained relatively low ever since. Only in Scotland was the further deceleration in growth rates in the 1970s and 1980s accompanied by a decline in the absolute size of the resident population in both decades.

With few exceptions, rates of population increase in Britain since the First World War have been lower and less volatile than in other European countries. Generally, however, the recent evolution of Britain's population has followed a pattern common to much of continental Europe. As in Britain, rates of population growth in most European states since 1918 have

Table 1.1 The population of England, Wales, Scotland and Britain, 1801–1991 (thousands[*])

	England	Wales	Scotland	Britain
1801	8305	587	1608	1 0500
1811	9491	673	1806	1 1970
1821	1 1206	794	2092	1 4092
1831	1 2992	904	2364	1 6260
1841	1 4868	1046	2620	1 8534
1851	1 6764	1163	2889	2 0816
1861	1 8780	1286	3062	2 3128
1871	2 1300	1412	3360	2 6072
1881	2 4403	1572	3736	2 9711
1891	2 7231	1771	4026	3 3028
1901	3 0515	2013	4472	3 7000
1911	3 3650	2421	4761	4 0832
1921	3 5230	2656	4882	4 2768
1931	3 7359	2593	4843	4 4795
1939	3 8995	2465	5007	4 6467
1951	4 1159	2599	5096	4 8854
1961	4 3461	2644	5179	5 1284
1971	4 6018	2731	5229	5 3978
1981	4 6226	2790	5131	5 4147
1991	4 6161	2799	4957	5 3917

[*] Excludes the Isle of Man, Jersey, Guernsey and associated islands.

Sources: Office of Population Censuses and Surveys (OPCS), *Census 1981. Historical Tables 1801–1981 England and Wales* (London, 1982), pp. 16–17. OPCS, *1991 Census. Preliminary Report for England and Wales* (London, 1991), p. 21.

fallen well below nineteenth-century levels and, apart from a handful of cases where the decline was reversed in the 1980s, fell continuously from the 1960s or 1970s onwards.[2] By the 1980s historically low rates of increase were the norm almost everywhere. In most countries population was growing more slowly than at any time since the early nineteenth century and in some rates of population growth barely exceeded the levels necessary for replacement.[3] Despite these broad similarities it bears emphasising that England and Scotland were the only European countries to experience absolute population

Table 1.2 The population of England, Wales, Scotland and Britain. Intercensal increase or decrease (–) (% per annum, 1801–1991[*])

	England	Wales	Scotland	Britain
1801–11	1.43	1.47	1.23	1.40
1811–21	1.81	1.79	1.58	1.77
1821–31	1.59	1.39	1.31	1.54
1831–41	1.44	1.57	1.08	1.40
1841–51	1.28	1.12	1.03	1.23
1851–61	1.14	1.01	0.58	1.11
1861–71	1.27	0.94	0.93	1.27
1871–81	1.47	1.07	1.06	1.40
1881–91	1.10	1.20	0.75	1.12
1891–1901	1.15	1.29	1.06	1.20
1901–11	0.98	1.86	0.63	1.04
1911–21	0.45	0.91	0.25	0.47
1921–31	0.60	–0.24	–0.08	0.47
1931–9	0.53	–0.62	0.41	0.47
1939–51	0.46	0.45	0.15	0.43
1951–61	0.54	0.17	0.16	0.50
1961–71	0.57	0.32	0.10	0.53
1971–81	0.05	0.22	–0.19	0.03
1981–91	–0.01	0.03	–0.34	–0.04

[*] Excludes the Isle of Man, Jersey, Guernsey and associated islands.
Sources: See Table 1.1.

decline during the 1980s while rates of population increase in Wales were also among the lowest recorded. Since 1918, indeed, Scottish and Welsh growth rates have been consistently among the slowest in Europe.

Regional Distribution

The twentieth-century trend towards lower and, ultimately, negligible or negative rates of population increase has been accompanied by major changes in the spatial distribution of Britain's inhabitants. The most significant alterations in *regional* patterns of residence are summarised in Table 1.3.

In some respects, it is true, the regional structure of Britain's population over the last two centuries has displayed a remarkable continuity. The share of the mainland population resident in England, for instance, has risen continuously from at least as early as the middle of the eighteenth century while that of Scotland and, until the 1970s, of Wales has steadily declined. Within England, where the South East remained the largest population concentration, followed invariably in the same order by the North West, the West Midlands and Yorkshire/Humberside, the North and East Midlands and East Anglia, the ranking of regions according to their share of total population changed little between 1801 and 1991. Only the South West, whose share fell from second or third largest in the first half of the nineteenth century to fifth largest in the twentieth, significantly altered its place in the regional ranking.

Recognition of these broad continuities in regional population distribution, however, must not be allowed to obscure the existence of important changes in residential location that have occurred around them. Between 1801 and 1911, for example, the Western Lowlands region of Scotland more than doubled its share of the nation's population while that of all other regions of the country declined, moderately in the cases of the Eastern Lowlands and the North East, more substantially in the Far North, the Highlands and the Borders. At a lesser pace the trend towards residence in the Western Lowlands continued throughout the interwar period, largely at the expense of the Far North, the Highlands and the North East. Between 1801 and 1939 the pecentage of Scotland's population living in the Western Lowlands (the counties of Ayr, Lanark and Renfrew) rose from a fifth to almost a half.[4] Since the Second World War it has declined slightly. But even as late as 1971, 43 per cent of all Scotland's inhabitants still resided in Western Lowland counties.

In England the regional distribution of residence had already begun to shift from south to north in the second half of the eighteenth century. Between 1751 and 1801 the North West, Yorkshire/Humberside and West Midlands regions increased their combined share of the country's population from 19.4 per cent to 24.4 per cent. The share of the population living in the East Midlands, East Anglia and the South West, on the other hand, fell from 27.9 per cent to 24.9 per cent. This northward drift persisted throughout much of the nineteenth century. By 1851, 29 per cent of the population of England lived in the North West, Yorkshire/Humberside and West Midland counties: by 1901, 31.9 per cent. In contrast the share of East Midland, East Anglian and South West counties fell to 21.3 per cent and 15.4 per cent. Had it not been for a persistent increase in the proportion of the population resident in the South East the south–north shift of residence in the eighteenth and nineteenth centuries would have been even more marked.

At the same time as the geography of England's population was drifting northwards the pattern of residence was altering in favour of central rather than more peripheral parts of Britain. Except for a few areas like central Scotland, South

Table 1.3 Percentage share of the population of mainland Britain, by region, 1751–1991

	1751	1801	1851	1901	1951	1961	1971	1981	1991
England	76.8	79.1	80.5	82.5	84.3	84.7	85.3	85.5	85.6
South East	22.8	23.8	24.6	28.4	31.0	31.2	32.0	30.9	31.0
West Midlands	7.5	8.2	8.2	8.1	9.1	9.3	9.5	9.5	9.4
East Midlands	6.4	6.1	5.5	5.4	5.9	6.5	6.3	7.0	7.2
East Anglia	6.5	6.0	5.0	3.1	2.8	2.9	3.1	3.4	3.7
South West	15.0	12.8	10.8	6.9	6.6	7.2	7.0	8.0	8.5
Yorkshire/ Humberside	6.2	7.8	8.7	9.5	9.3	9.1	8.9	9.0	8.8
North West	5.7	8.4	12.1	14.3	13.2	12.5	12.5	11.8	11.4
North	6.7	6.0	5.6	6.8	6.4	6.1	6.1	5.7	5.6
Wales	6.1	5.6	5.6	5.4	5.3	5.2	5.0	5.2	5.2
Scotland	17.1	15.3	13.9	12.1	10.4	10.1	9.7	9.5	9.2

Sources: R. Lawton, 'Regional Population Trends in England and Wales, 1750–1971', in J. Hobcraft and P. Rees (eds), *Regional Demographic Development* (London, 1978), p. 36. OPCS, *1991 Census. Preliminary Report for England and Wales* (London, 1991), p. 33.

Wales and North East England where rates of population growth remained high, the regions of most rapid population increase before 1914 were located in a belt of core counties stretching from South Lancashire and West Yorkshire through the East Midlands to Greater London. Between 1851 and 1911 fewer than a third of all registration districts in England and Wales, most of them lying in central locations, had rates of population growth above the national average. In as many as a third of all English and Welsh registration districts, the majority situated in geographically more peripheral areas, the absolute number of inhabitants actually decreased.

Even before the outbreak of the First World War, however, the tendency for Britain's population to drift from south to north and from periphery to core was beginning to slacken. By the interwar period new patterns of regional population growth and distribution, involving a reversal of the south–north drift and a slowing down in the relocation of people from peripheral to core regions, had emerged. During the 1920s and 1930s the only regions of England to experience rates of population growth in excess of the national average were the South East and the West and East Midlands. Compared with the period before 1914 the pace of population growth in the North, North West and Yorkshire/Humberside regions was now relatively low and whereas many peripheral areas, particularly in remoter northern and western parts, continued to record some of the heaviest population losses, others, especially in East Anglia and the South West, experienced rates of population increase that differed little from those of the North, North West and Yorkshire/Humberside.[5]

The reversal of nineteenth-century regional patterns of population growth and distribution has persisted in the second half of the twentieth century. During the 1950s and early 1960s the continuing north to south residential drift was reflected in relatively high rates of population growth in all regions of the south and the midlands, including the South East (Table 1.4). Even as late as the period 1961–6 rates of population increase in the South East remained above the average for Britain as a whole and were only slightly lower than those in East Anglia, the South West and the East Midlands, the regions of most rapid growth.[6] Throughout the 1970s and 1980s, despite a modest contribution from the South East in the years 1977–84, the southwards shift of residence remained chiefly a redistribution towards East Anglia, the South West and the East Midlands. Between the First World War and the mid 1960s the drift south was predominantly a movement towards counties in the South East and the West Midlands. After the mid 1960s it was directed primarily at those in East Anglia, the South East and the East Midlands.[7]

As indicated by the persistence of relatively high rates of population growth in regions like East Anglia and the South West, the decades since the Second World War also experienced a moderate transfer of people from core to more peripheral parts of the country. By the 1970s and 1980s rates of population growth in many of the remoter parts of Britain – west, middle and north Wales, northern Scotland and the Scottish borders, Cumbria, north Yorkshire and elsewhere in

Table 1.4 Intercensal rates of population growth in Britain by region, 1951–1991 (%)

	1951–61	1961–71	1971–81	1981–91
England	5.6	5.7	0.5	−0.1
North	3.2	0.7	−1.4	−3.0
Yorkshire/Humberside	2.3	3.7	−0.1	−1.8
North West	1.9	2.6	−2.9	−4.3
East Midlands	7.6	9.4	4.8	2.5
West Midlands	7.6	7.4	0.5	−1.4
East Anglia	5.2	13.6	11.7	7.7
South East	7.5	5.9	−1.2	−0.1
South West	5.8	10.6	6.0	5.5
Scotland	1.6	1.0	−1.9	−3.4
Wales	1.7	3.2	2.2	0.3

Sources: A. G. Champion, 'Population Trends in the 1970s', in J. B. Goddard and A. G. Champion (eds), *The Urban and Regional Transformation of Britain* (London, 1983), p. 197. B. R. Mitchell and H. G. Jones, *Second Abstract of British Historical Statistics* (Cambridge, 1971), pp. 16–17. OPCS, *1991 Census. Preliminary Report for England and Wales* (London, 1991), pp. 3, 21.

northern England, Cambridgeshire, Cornwall, Devon, Dorset, Norfolk, Somerset, Suffolk and Wiltshire – were among the highest achieved anywhere.[8] Typical of what happened in many outlying areas was the experience of the Highlands and Islands region of Scotland where, after a century of persistent decline, the number of inhabitants increased in the 1960s and 1970s.[9]

Urbanisation

Changes in the regional distribution of residence have been accompanied by equally pronounced changes in the relative extent of urban and rural living.

The bulk of the transformation from rural to urban residence occurred in the nineteenth century. In Scotland the proportion of the population living in communities of 5000 inhabitants or more rose from 21 per cent in 1801 to over 58 per cent in 1911, with the Western and Eastern Lowlands accounting for more than four in every five urban dwellers.[10] In England and Wales the urban population rose from 24 per cent of the total in 1750 to almost 34 per cent in 1801 before accelerating to 54 per cent by 1851 and 79 per cent by 1911.[11] On the eve of the First World War Britain had already become the world's first extensively urbanised society. The trend towards urban living has continued ever since, though inevitably at a much slower pace. By 1981 the share of the British population in communities with at least 2000 inhabitants had risen to over 89 per cent.[12]

The most intriguing feature of the history of urbanisation in the twentieth century, however, is what has happened to the size of the very largest urban communities.

At the beginning of the nineteenth century London was the only place in Britain with a population in excess of 100 000. By 1851 the number of communities with populations of 100 000 or more had risen to 10, by 1911 to 39 and by 1951 to 59.[13] By this stage the density of urban concentration in certain parts of the country was sufficient to persuade the Registrar-General to distinguish seven conurbation areas – Greater London,

Merseyside, South East Lancashire, Tyneside, the West Midlands and West Yorkshire in England, and Clydeside in Scotland. As early as 1901 these together accounted for almost 40 per cent of Britain's total population. By 1961 the figure had reached 42 per cent. Thereafter it began to decline, to under 39 per cent in 1971, around 36 per cent in 1981 and under 35 per cent in 1991. The trend away from conurbation residence was common to all conurbations. In the case of South East Lancashire (Greater Manchester), with a brief interruption in the 1950s, it began as early as the second decade of the century: in Clydeside and Greater London from the 1930s: in Merseyside, Tyneside and the West Midlands from the 1960s. Only in the case of the Yorkshire conurbations of Leeds and Sheffield was it barely noticeable.

Indications of a growing preference for life in smaller, less densely populated settlements were already apparent in the 1950s. Although the populations of the inner, core districts of the largest urban communities continued to increase, their rate of increase was lower than that in surrounding suburban areas. In some instances, a few dating back to the early years of the century, the populations of inner city districts even declined absolutely. Though growth rates in metropolitan regions during the 1950s were still above those in non-metropolitan rural regions, where the number of inhabitants continued to fall, they were now no higher than the average for Britain as a whole and distinctly lower than those in non-metropolitan urban regions. For the first time the traditional, positive correlation between settlement size and rate of population growth in some cases began to give way to a negative correlation.[14]

Between 1961 and the mid 1970s the trend towards population deconcentration intensified dramatically.[15] As Table 1.5 shows, the main loci of population growth shifted from metropolitan to non-metropolitan, or freestanding, regions and, within each type of region, from urban cores to less urbanised surrounds.

In the 1960s the population of Greater London decreased at an accelerating rate and much more rapidly than that of other metropolitan regions in England and Wales, where numbers

even rose slightly during the first half of the decade. In stark
contrast the populations of non-metropolitan regions increased
substantially. Within both metropolitan and non-metropolitan
regions there was a steady drift of population away from the
most densely settled areas. In the Greater London Metropolitan
District the loss of population was more pronounced in inner
than outer areas. In other metropolitan districts there was a
marked distinction between the experience of the principal
cities, whose populations declined,[16] and that of their surrounding areas, whose populations continued to grow. By the end of
the decade the share of urban core populations in the total
population of all metropolitan regions had been greatly
reduced.[17]

A similar trend towards a less centralised pattern of residence occurred in non-metropolitan regions. In the course of
the second half of the 1960s a modest increase in the size of
non-metropolitan city populations gave way to a modest
decrease. Throughout the decade rates of population growth
in non-metropolitan cities fell well below those in other parts
of the non-metropolitan regions. It was in new towns like
Basildon and Stevenage and in medium-sized or small urban
communities like Bristol, Leicester and Southampton that the
highest rates of population growth in Britain were attained.[18]
Rates of population increase in excess of the national average
and comfortably above those in metropolitan regions and
cities generally were also recorded in port, resort and retirement settlements and in industrial and remoter, largely rural
parts of non-metropolitan regions. The demographic experience of the more remote, rural areas of England and Wales
during the 1960s is particularly striking. In the 1950s these
had continued to lose population. In some cases, in parts of
Wales and along the Welsh and Scottish borders for instance,
the decline in population persisted into the early 1960s. By the
end of the decade, however, decline had been replaced by
growth. In contrast to what happened elsewhere in England
and Wales rates of population increase in remoter, largely
rural districts were higher between 1966 and 1971 than
between 1961 and 1966.[19]

The spatial redistribution of population which occurred in Britain between the 1950s and 1960s was essentially a flight from the cities or, more precisely, from their high-density, inner cores. The new pattern emerged first and proceeded most rapidly in the largest cities but ultimately affected all city populations. In the course of the 1960s the aggregate population of the seven principal cities of England and Wales fell by over 8 per cent and that of the ten large cities by over 1 per cent. The total population of the 16 smaller cities, on the other hand, rose by more than 2 per cent. Only five of the country's smaller cities experienced a decline in population between 1966 and 1971. Despite this the growth of even small city populations remained well below that of most other urban and rural communities.[20]

The process of decentralisation reached its peak in the early 1970s. Between 1971 and 1974 the drain of population from metropolitan regions and from the cities of non-metropolitan regions was as high or higher than at any time during the previous decade. By contrast rates of population growth elsewhere remained substantially positive. The result was that the difference between the demographic experience of metropolitan and non-metropolitan regions widened. Within the Greater London metropolis population losses were more severe in inner than outer boroughs; in other metropolitan regions more severe in the principal cities than elsewhere. Within non-metropolitan regions too rates of population growth were negative in the cities and, except in the new towns, lower in urban and industrial than in remoter, largely rural areas, the only type of district to boast higher rates of increase in the early 1970s than in the 1960s.[21]

Even in the early 1970s, however, there were signs that the pace of decentralisation was about to slow. In Greater London the acceleration in rates of population decline was more marked in outer than inner boroughs; in other metropolitan regions greater in 'other districts' than in the principal cities, while in non-metropolitan regions rates of population growth rose in remote, rural areas and stabilised in the cities but fell elsewhere. After the mid 1970s, although the process of decentralisation continued, it did so at a slower and generally diminishing pace. By the late 1980s variations in rates of population growth from one type of district to another were negligible.

From its peak in the mid 1970s the pace of population decline in the Greater London metropolis progressively lessened. Between 1984 and 1987, for the first time in over 30 years, the population of Greater London rose. Significantly, when it once more began to decline in the late 1980s, the decline was much less pronounced than that of the 1960s and 1970s. Population losses in other metropolitan regions during the late 1980s were likewise less severe than at any time since the early 1970s. In non-metropolitan regions, on the other hand, rates of population growth between 1974/7 and 1988/91 were lower than in the 1960s and early 1970s. As a result, over the period 1974/7–1988/91 the differential in rates of population growth between metropolitan and non-metropolitan regions steadily narrowed until by the close of the period the populations of both regions were declining at much the same pace.[22]

Further evidence of the recent downturn in the speed of decentralisation is provided by the changes that have occurred in the spatial distribution of residence *within* metropolitan and non-metropolitan regions. In the Greater London metropolis the contrasts between the demographic evolution of inner and outer boroughs were much less marked by the 1980s. By 1988–91, indeed, the population of inner London was falling no more rapidly than that of outer London. In other metropolitan regions, though losses of population from the principal cities continued to exceed those elsewhere, the differentials similarly narrowed after the mid 1970s and by 1988–91 were smaller than at any time since the early 1960s. In non-metropolitan regions the recent evolution of residential patterns has been more complex. But here too the general tendency has been towards a reduction in the pace of dispersal. Before the late 1980s the extent of the reduction was modest. Between 1974/7 and 1984/7 non-metropolitan cities continued to lose residents to all other types of settlement except the industrial. Broadly, however, the scale of the loss was smaller than in the 1960s and early 1970s. The extent to which rates of population growth in new town, other urban and remoter, largely rural areas exceeded the non-metropolitan average declined from the mid 1970s. Only in port, resort and retirement areas did rates of growth exceed the non-metropolitan average by a wider margin between 1981/4 and 1984/7 than in the previous 20 years. In non-metropolitan regions the trend away from residential dispersal suddenly and sharply intensified in the late 1980s. By 1991, in metropolitan and non-metropolitan regions alike, rates of population growth varied little from one type of district to another. Never before had there been such uniformity in the geography of population trends.[23]

Inevitably, as the rate of regional population dispersal slowed, so did the rate of counterurbanisation. Throughout the 1970s, it is true, the redistribution of people from larger to smaller urban communities and from urban to rural areas continued and there remained a strong, negative overall correlation between rates of population growth and settlement size. Population losses were still heaviest in the largest cities and diminished or gave way to population gains as the size of settlement decreased.[24] But a significant change was already beginning to occur. From the middle years of the decade the pace of population decline in London and other principal cities and of population increase in new town, port, resort, retirement and rural settlements started to slow. By the end of the decade variations in rates of population growth between settlements of different size had narrowed perceptibly.[25]

The pace of counterurbanisation slowed further in the 1980s. Although the populations of the cities and largest towns continued to decline, they did so at a noticeably slower rate than in the 1970s. The rate of decline in the population of the London boroughs fell from −10 per cent between 1971 and 1981 to less than −5 per cent between 1981 and 1991: in the principal cities of other metropolitan regions from −10 per cent to just over −7 per cent: in non-metropolitan cities from under −5 to around −2 per cent: and in non-metropolitan large towns from −5 to well under −4 per cent. By comparison, in most other types of settlement demographic circumstances worsened between the 1970s and 1980s. In non-metropolitan regions the growth rate of small towns fell from 3.5 to 0.3 per cent, of industrial districts from about 3 to –0.2 per cent, of new town districts from about 15 to 6 per cent, of other urban and mixed urban-rural districts from between 7 and 8 per cent to between 3 and 4 per cent and of remoter, largely rural communities from over 10 per cent to between 6 and 7 per cent. Except for cities and large towns the only settlement type to improve its demographic profile between the two decades was the resort, port and retirement districts where rates of population growth rose from just under 5 per cent in the 1970s to just over 5 per cent in the 1980s.[26] In the course of the period 1971/8–1978/84 the largest upward shifts in population growth rates occurred in the inner London boroughs, in other major cities like Birmingham, Glasgow, Liverpool and Manchester and in seaside resorts like Bournemouth, Hastings and Hove. New and expanded towns such as Cramlington, Cumbernauld, East Kilbride, Runcorn, Skelmersdale, Tamworth, Telford and Thetford and some of the more remote rural areas like Nairn, Radnor, Ross and the Shetlands, by contrast, experienced particularly sharp declines in rates of population increase.[27]

Despite its slackening pace the trend away from residence in the largest, most densely populated settlements persisted more or less throughout the 1980s.[28] As Table 1.5 shows, it was not until 1988–91 that variations in rates of population growth between different types of settlement practically disappeared. The effective culmination of the tendency towards residential deconcentration has been a very recent phenomenon.

Allowing for some variation in timing, extent and occasionally even direction, the changes that have taken place in the geography of human residence in Britain in recent decades have been shared by most countries of the advanced world. From the USA and Canada through the countries of non-Communist Europe to countries like Australia and Japan an established preference for life in densely populated urban areas gave way to a preference for less urbanised and more

Table 1.5 Average annual rates of population growth by type of district. England and Wales 1961–1991 (per thousand population)

	1961–6	1966–71	1971–4	1974–7	1977–81	1981–4	1984–7	1988–91
Greater London	-4	-9	-12	-12	-7	-2	1	-2
Inner London	-8	-19	-21	-19	-15	-5	0	-2
Outer London	-1	-2	-6	-7	-3	-1	-2	-2
Metropolitan Districts	2	-0	-4	-5	-4	-4	-3	-1
Principal cities	-8	-8	-11	-10	-8	-5	-2	-2
Other districts	7	4	-1	0	-3	-3	6	-1
Non-Metropolitan Districts	13	10	8	5	5	3	4	-1
Cities	1	-2	-2	-3	-3	-3	-4	-1
Industrial	8	7	7	1	2	-1	1	-0
With new towns	23	19	16	14	14	8	9	-0
Resort, port, retirement	14	10	9	5	5	5	13	-1
Other urban	23	17	9	6	7	5	7	-0
Remoter, largely rural	8	10	15	9	7	6	11	-0
England and Wales	6	4	2	0	1	1	3	-1

Sources: A. G. Champion, 'United Kingdom: Population Deconcentration as a Cyclic Phenomenon', in A. G. Champion (ed.), *Counterurbanization. The Changing Pace and Nature of Population Deconcentration* (London, 1989), p. 91. C. Jones and Bob Armitage, 'Population Change within Area Types: England and Wales, 1971–88', *Population Trends*, 60 (1990), 25. OPCS, *1991 Census. Preliminary Report for England and Wales* (London, 1991), p. 6.

scattered patterns of residence. Throughout the developed world the 1970s was characterised by unprecedented rates of population deconcentration as people deserted the inner cities for the suburbs, large cities for smaller cities and towns, metropolitan for non-metropolitan locations, and urban for rural environments. By the 1980s, just as they did in Britain, so almost everywhere in the developed world the closely associated processes of decentralisation and counterurbanisation slowed down.[29] It follows that whatever factors were responsible for recent changes in the internal geography of Britain's population must also have been active elsewhere.

Summary

Perhaps the most striking contrast between the demographic structures of nineteenth- and twentieth-century Britain is the dramatic decline which occurred in rates of population growth after 1911. Almost the whole of this decline occurred in two decades – the 1910s, when rates of population growth slumped to less than half those of the decades immediately preceding the First World War, and the 1970s, when after half a century of relative stability rates of population increase fell to levels barely above and subsequently below replacement. High rates of population growth between the late eighteenth and early twentieth centuries were accompanied by a shift in the distribution of residence from peripheral to core regions and from south to north. Lower rates of population growth after the First World War, on the other hand, were accompanied by a redistribution of residence in favour of the periphery rather than the core and the south at the expense of the north. At the same time, although the nineteenth-century tendency for people to concentrate in conurbations continued throughout the first half of the twentieth century, the period since the 1960s and early 1970s has been characterised by a flight from conurbation residence and by a preference for less densely populated habitats – in non-metropolitan rather than metropolitan regions and in smaller urban and rural settlements rather than cities and larger towns. The pace of this residential dispersal, however, had already begun to slow down by the late 1970s and by the end of the 1980s had almost entirely ceased.

Underlying these changes in national and regional rates of population growth and residential distribution was a complex interplay of the forces of migration, mortality and fertility and the factors responsible for shaping them. The behaviour of these mechanisms and their determining influences will be examined in the subsequent chapters.

2

INTERNAL AND OVERSEAS MIGRATION

The trends in national and regional rates of population growth summarised in the previous chapter were the result of changes in rates of natural increase (defined as the relationship between numbers of births and deaths) and in the balance between in- and out-migration. The relative significance of each of these variables has varied greatly both over time and from place to place.

For England and Wales and mainland Britain as a whole rates of population growth from at least as early as the mid sixteenth century have been determined chiefly by fluctuations in levels of natural increase. Between the 1560s and 1640s net out-migration removed no more than a fifth of England's excess of births over deaths. Between the 1690s and 1710s the proportion rose to just over a quarter. From the 1730s to the 1860s it averaged less than a tenth. Only between the 1650s and 1680s and again in the 1720s did rates of English population growth prior to the middle of the nineteenth century owe more to the influence of net migration than natural increase.[1]

Natural increase has remained the predominant mechanism of overall English and British population trends ever since. Except for the occasional year, at no time from the 1870s to the 1980s did the net gain or loss of people on balance of migration play more than a minor role in altering the size of

19

Britain's population. In the 1870s, 1890s and 1950s rates of British population growth were determined almost entirely by variations in rates of natural increase. In the 1880s, 1900s, 1920s–1940s and 1960s the contribution of net migration, though never more than modest, was somewhat greater. Only during the 1910s, 1970s and 1980s, when the net loss on migration amounted to around one-third of the excess of births over deaths, was it more substantial. But even in these decades changes in the relative levels of fertility and mortality exercised the dominant influence (Table 2.1).[2]

In the case of Scotland, at least in recent times, the impact of net migration on rates of population growth has been more pronounced. Before the 1770s levels of net out-migration from Scotland were negligible and rates of population growth dependent almost entirely on variations in rates of natural increase. Even during the later decades of the eighteenth century, when the number of Scots leaving for overseas destinations rose, net out-migration reduced the excess of births

Table 2.1 Net migration as a percentage of natural increase. Great Britain, 1871–1991

1871–81	−6.6
1881–91	−19.8
1891–1901	−3.0
1901–11	−16.5
1911–21	−30.7
1921–31	−21.7
1931–51	+15.2
1951–61	+5.1
1961–71	−12.6
1971–81	−30.6
1981–91	+36.0

Sources: Registrar-General Scotland, *Annual Report 1971. Part II – Population and Vital Statistics* (Edinburgh, 1972), p. 43. Registrar-General England and Wales, *Statistical Review for 1971. Part II. Tables. Population* (London, 1973), p. 89. OPCS, *International Migration 1980. United Kingdom, England and Wales* (London, 1981), p. 11. OPCS, *International Migration 1991. United Kingdom. England and Wales* (London, 1993), p. 1.

over deaths by only 15 per cent. Between 1825 and 1853 the proportion of the country's natural surplus leaving Scottish ports for overseas destinations, the principal outlets for Scottish emigrants at the time, remained below a fifth. Beginning around the middle years of the nineteenth century the contribution of net out-migration to rates of Scottish population growth increased dramatically. Between the 1860s and the end of the 1930s over half of Scotland's surplus of births over deaths was lost on balance of migration, the ratio varying positively with fluctuations in the volume of emigration from as little as 10 per cent in the 1890s and about 20 per cent in the 1870s and 1930s, to between 40 per cent and 50 per cent in the 1880s and 1900s, 66 per cent in the 1910s and 111 per cent in the 1920s and generally reaching higher levels in the first half of the twentieth century than in the second half of the nineteenth. After the Second World War the contribution of net out-migration to Scottish population growth increased still further. Between the 1950s and 1960s the proportion of the country's natural surplus lost to net emigration rose from three-quarters to over four-fifths. By the 1970s the excess of emigrants over immigrants was two to three times larger than the excess of births over deaths: by the 1980s four to five times larger (Table 2.2).[3] Before the 1920s most Scottish emigrants went overseas rather than to other parts of the United Kingdom. During the interwar period this pattern was reversed, more than four-fifths of the net outflow, initially at least, departing for United Kingdom destinations. After the Second World War a preference for overseas destinations re-emerged and the number of Scottish emigrants going to other parts of the United Kingdom declined to between a third and a half of the total.[4]

Until well into the twentieth century rates of population growth within the different regions and settlement types of each country on the British mainland were also determined chiefly by the behaviour of natural increase. In Scotland this remained the case until the second half of the century. In no decade between the 1860s and 1930s did migrational balances raise or lower regional Scottish population totals by much

Table 2.2 Net migration as a percentage of natural increase. Scotland 1861–1990

1861–71	–28.5
1871–81	–19.9
1881–91	–42.9
1891–1901	–10.7
1901–11	–46.8
1911–21	–66.2
1921–31	–111.2
1931–51	–49.6
1951–61	–75.6
1961–71	–85.6
1971–81	–267.7
1981–90	–468.7

Source: Registrar-General Scotland, *Annual Report* 1990 (Edinburgh, 1991), p. 107.

more than a tenth, and typically by a good deal less.[5] In more recent decades, however, the contribution of net migration to changes in the size of the population in a number of Scottish regions has greatly increased. By the 1960s, as was the case in other remote, rural areas of Britain and elsewhere in the developed world, migration had already become the main determinant of population growth in the Scottish Highlands and Islands. By the 1970s it was the dominant force in the Borders, Fife, Grampian, Strathclyde and Tayside, as well as in the Highlands and the islands of Orkney and Shetland. In the Western Isles net migration and natural increase contributed more or less equally to population growth. Only in the Central, Dumfries/Galloway and Lothian regions were variations in the number of inhabitants still determined primarily by trends in rates of natural increase. By the 1980s natural increase remained the principal mechanism of population change in the Lothians and had become the dominant influence in Fife, Tayside and the Western Isles. Elsewhere – in the Borders, Central, Dumfries/Galloway, Grampian, the Highlands, Orkney/Shetland and Strathclyde – migration played the key role.[6]

In England and Wales too regional rates of population growth prior to the First World War owed far more to the influence of natural increase than to that of net migration. Thereafter the relative contribution of the two variables changed. As early as the 1920s net migration had become the main determinant of population growth in almost two-thirds of all urban and over three-quarters of all rural areas. By the 1950s and 1960s a clear distinction had emerged between the experiences of regions in the southern and northern halves of England. In the former, comprising the Greater London, Outer Metropolitan, Outer South East, East Anglian and South West regions, gains or, in the case of Greater London, losses on balance of in- and out-migration were the chief cause of variations in population size. In the latter, comprising the East and West Midlands, the North, North West and Yorkshire/Humberside, trends in natural increase exerted the dominant influence.[7] By the 1970s and 1980s, as levels of natural increase continued to decline, rates of population growth in almost all regions of the country, particularly in metropolitan areas, came to depend predominantly on the effects of net migration.[8]

Focusing solely on the contribution of net migration to rates of population growth within individual regions and settlement types, moreover, does not do adequate justice to its importance. In the absence of substantial differences in rates of natural increase between regions, migration has always taken the leading role in determining regional differentials in population growth rates and thus in determining the changes which have occurred in the spatial distribution of Britain's inhabitants.

Even before 1914 regional differentials in rates of population increase in most cases depended far more on variations in the balance between in- and out-migration than on variations in the relationship between numbers of births and deaths. Most of the more striking features of regional differentials in rates of population growth during the interwar period – the abnormally high rates of growth in parts of the English Midlands, on Severnside and everywhere in South East

England except Inner London, and the higher rates of growth in southern than northern Britain – were also largely the result of differentials in migration balances.[9] After the Second World War migration remained the principal mechanism of regional differences in growth rates. Occasions when differentials in natural increase exercised an equal or greater influence on the geography of Britain's population were rare.[10] In the main it was through the agency of migration that variations in rates of population growth from one area to another were brought about.[11]

If then we are to explain the processes of decentralisation and counterurbanisation which occurred in twentieth-century Britain, and the north to south shift in residential distribution which accompanied them, it is to migration, and the forces responsible for it, that we must primarily turn. Chronological changes in rates of population growth, on the other hand, have more often been determined by the behaviour of natural increase. Yet even here there have been times when alterations in the balance of migration had a not insignificant impact.

Overseas Migration

For the period before 1912, when for the first time travellers between the United Kingdom and countries outside Europe were required to state whether or not they intended a permanent change of residence, reliable data on the extent of migration into and out of Britain are difficult to provide. Down to the middle of the nineteenth century it is probably safe to assume that the number of genuine emigrants and immigrants equated reasonably closely with the number of passengers travelling to and from non-European destinations. If this assumption is correct, compared with what was to follow the volume of in- and out-migration was as yet moderate. Over the whole of the seventeenth and eighteenth centuries the total number of emigrants from mainland Britain barely exceeded one million. Between 1815 and 1850 the scale of the exodus increased. In the second quarter of the nineteenth century alone at least half a million natives of England and Wales and a further 174 000 who left from Scottish ports emigrated overseas.[12] Altogether, between 1815 and 1850 around three-quarters of a million people born on the British mainland moved to non-European destinations.[13]

Until late in the eighteenth century levels of immigration were probably even lower than those of emigration.[14] As in the case of emigration, however, in the course of the late eighteenth and first half of the nineteenth centuries immigrant numbers began to rise, largely as a result of a growing influx from Ireland.[15] Despite this the volume of movement to mainland Britain in the mid nineteenth century was modest compared with what was to follow.

Data on numbers of passengers between the United Kingdom and extra-European countries imply that the scale of both emigration and immigration increased enormously between the middle of the nineteenth century and the outbreak of the First World War, with especially dramatic surges in emigration during the years 1879–93 and 1903–14. Because of an increase in the amount of intercontinental travel for reasons of business or pleasure, made possible by improvements in methods of overseas transport, a close equation between numbers of passengers and numbers of genuine migrants can no longer be assumed. It follows that the absolute volumes of emigration and immigration in the half century or so preceding the First World War cannot be quantified with any precision. Fortunately, since the numbers of people moving into and out of the country for business or pleasure purposes were roughly similar the early passenger statistics can be regarded as a reasonably accurate guide to the balance between in- and out-migration.

A comparison of passenger statistics for United Kingdom citizens in the decades before 1913 with migration statistics for British citizens in subsequent decades suggests that in the years immediately following the First World War the scale of emigration reached levels not far short of those attained during the great prewar peaks of 1879–93 and 1903–14. In the second half of the 1920s rates of emigration fell to the much lower levels prevalent in the third quarter of the nineteenth century and between 1894 and 1902. They fell even more dramatically at the start of the 1930s and remained at very low levels throughout the decade. After the Second World War emigrant totals once more rose and have stayed at levels similar to those of the 1920s ever since. In every decade from

Table 2.3 Number of migrants by sea between the United Kingdom and non-European countries, 1913, 1920–1963 (thousands*)

	In	Out	Balance
1913	85.7	389.4	−303.7
1920	86.1	285.1	−199.0
1921	71.4	199.5	−128.1
1922	68.0	174.1	−106.1
1923	57.6	256.3	−198.7
1924	64.1	155.4	−91.3
1925	56.3	140.6	−84.3
1926	51.1	166.6	−115.5
1927	55.7	153.5	−97.8
1928	59.1	136.8	−77.8
1929	56.2	143.7	−87.5
1930	66.2	92.9	−26.7
1920–30	691.8	1904.5	−1212.7
1931	71.4	34.3	37.1
1932	75.6	27.0	48.6
1933	59.3	26.3	33.0
1934	49.8	29.2	20.6
1935	46.2	29.8	16.4
1936	47.2	29.8	17.4
1937	42.6	31.8	10.8
1938	40.6	34.1	6.5
1931–8	432.7	242.3	190.4
1946	63.1	166.6	−103.5
1947	56.5	121.6	−65.1
1948	73.7	168.1	−94.4
1949	64.8	152.6	−87.8
1950	71.9	136.3	−64.4

Table 2.3 *Continued*

	In	Out	Balance
1946–50	330.0	745.2	–415.2
1951	76.2	169.6	–93.4
1952	82.2	181.8	–99.6
1953	77.8	155.1	–77.3
1954	92.3	148.4	–56.1
1955	84.8	128.1	–43.3
1956	73.8	140.9	–67.1
1957	63.4	162.9	–99.5
1958	66.9	113.0	–46.1
1959	71.6	101.4	–29.8
1960	84.7	93.2	–8.5
1961	83.7	91.0	–7.3
1962	68.0	91.2	–23.2
1963	47.1	107.2	–60.1
1951–63	972.5	1683.8	–711.3

* From 1 April 1923 the figures exclude passengers arriving at and departing from ports in the Irish Free State. Before 1948 the data are for British citizens only. Migrants are defined as persons claiming a permanent change in country of residence.

Source: B. Thomas, *Migration and Economic Growth. A Study of Great Britain and the Atlantic Economy* (Cambridge, 1954), pp. 276–7. Central Statistical Office (CSO), *Annual Abstract of Statistics 1958* (London, 1958), p. 43. CSO, *Annual Abstract of Statistics 1962* (London, 1962), p. 40. CSO, *Annual Abstract of Statistics 1965* (London, 1965), p. 19.

the 1950s to the 1980s around 2 million people have left the United Kingdom to take up permanent residence elsewhere.

Trends in the volume of immigration followed a similar if less volatile pattern. As with emigration, the scale of immigration was greater in the years before and immediately after the First World War than in the second half of the 1920s and throughout the 1930s. On the other hand, the decline in immigration during the interwar period, particularly during the 1930s, was less marked than that in emigration. Indeed, in contrast to the number of emigrants, immigrant numbers in the early 1930s exceeded those in most years of the previous decade. After the Second World War the volume of immigration, like that of emigration, considerably increased. Even allowing for the fact that earlier data exclude non-British citizens, the number of migrants coming to the United Kingdom by sea from countries outside Europe was greater between 1946 and 1963 than at any time since the early 1930s. After the mid 1960s it rose to levels greater than at any time since statistics on migration first began to be formally recorded.

Until 1914 migrants to Britain were drawn mainly from Ireland and Eastern Europe. Large-scale immigration from Ireland originated in the late eighteenth century and peaked in the 1840s and 1850s. From then until the outbreak of the First World War the volume of Irish immigration declined to a relative trickle and, though still the largest foreign-born group, the share of Irish-born in the total population of mainland Britain steadily decreased.[16] Immigration from Russia and other parts of Eastern Europe, predominantly of Jews, first became extensive in the early 1880s and reached its highest levels between 1899 and 1905/6. Between two-thirds and three-quarters of the 250 000 or so Jews resident in England and Wales in 1914, when Russian and Eastern European immigrants accounted for nearly one-third of all foreign-born inhabitants, had entered the country at some time during the previous 25 years. By comparison, the volume of immigration from other sources was as yet small: a handful of Chinese living in London and the principal sea ports; a small but growing number of blacks from Africa and the Caribbean; and slightly larger numbers of Americans, French, Germans and Italians and other white immigrants from Australia, Canada, New Zealand and South Africa.[17]

Throughout the interwar period Jewish immigrants, now drawn mainly from Germany and elsewhere in central Europe, continued to contribute substantially to United Kingdom immigration flows, particularly during the 1930s when at least 60 000 came to settle. But the chief sources of immigration in the decades between the two world wars were the Irish Republic, which supplied a net influx of over 239 000 immi-

Table 2.4 Number of migrants into and out of the United
Kingdom by sea and air, 1964–1990 (thousands*)

	In	Out	Balance
1964	214	273	–59
1965	211	288	–77
1966	222	304	–82
1967	236	322	–86
1968	237	281	–44
1969	222	299	–77
1970	226	291	–65
1964–70	1568	2058	–490
1971	200	240	–40
1972	222	233	–11
1973	196	246	–50
1974	184	269	–85
1975	197	238	–41
1976	191	210	–19
1977	163	209	–46
1978	187	192	–5
1979	195	189	6
1980	173	228	–55
1971–80	1908	2254	–346
1981	153	232	–79
1982	201	257	–56
1983	202	184	17
1984	201	164	37
1985	232	174	58
1986	250	213	37
1987	211	209	2
1988	216	237	–21
1989	250	205	45
1990	267	231	36
1981–90	2183	2106	77

* The figures are estimates devised from the International Passenger
  Survey, a sample survey covering the main air and sea routes between the
  United Kingdom and all overseas destinations except the Irish Republic.
  They include people subject to immigration controls as well as British
  citizens. Migrants are defined as persons who have lived either in the
  United Kingdom or abroad for at least one year and who declare an
  intention to live elsewhere for at least one year.

Sources: CSO, *Annual Abstract of Statistics 1971* (London, 1971), p. 21. CSO,
  Annual Abstract of Statistics 1981 (London, 1981), p. 26. CSO,
  Annual Abstract of Statistics 1992 (London, 1992), p. 19.

grants between 1924 and 1939, and, in the 1930s, 'New World' countries like Canada and the USA from which earlier British emigrants returned in large numbers. Coloured immigration from Africa, the Caribbean and the Indian sub-continent remained negligible.[18]

Apart from its increasing scale, the most striking feature of United Kingdom immigration in the second half of the twentieth century has been the emergence of the Caribbean islands and the Indian sub-continent as major immigrant sources.

The arrival of nearly 500 immigrants from Jamaica in 1948 is usually regarded as the start of the great postwar surge in coloured immigration. In fact, as late as 1952 and 1953 the annual inflow of migrants from the West Indies still barely exceeded 2000. In 1954, partly due to restrictions on West Indian migration to the USA following the McCarran–Walter Act of 1952, the number of West Indians migrating to Britain suddenly rose to over 9000. By 1961 it had risen to over 74 000. Between 1952 and 1961, when coloured immigration was dominated by people of West Indian origin, a total of almost 290 000 people came from the islands of the Caribbean to settle in Britain. In subsequent years both the absolute and relative volume of West Indian immigration decreased. By 1966 numbers had fallen to 15 000, by 1971 to 5000 and from 1976 onwards to no more than 3000 or 4000 a year.

Beginning in the early 1960s, immigrants from the Caribbean were replaced by immigrants from the Indian sub-continent as the main source of coloured immigration. First significant in 1953, the number of arrivals from the Indian sub-continent increased from around 11 000 in 1955 to between 70 000 and 100 000 a year by the early 1960s. As with West Indian immigration, the scale of the influx subsequently declined, to an annual average of about 27 000 in the mid 1960s and mid 1970s, and 25 000 or 26 000 between 1981 and 1986. Not even the arrival of over 111 000 Asian immigrants from Kenya and Uganda between 1968 and 1975 did more than temporarily halt the decline which occurred in the absolute and relative size of coloured immigration from its early 1960s peak.[19]

For all its size and novelty coloured immigration was by no means the only nor, except for brief periods, even the main type of immigration to Britain in the second half of the twentieth century. Between 1945 and the late 1950s more than a third of a million immigrants came from continental Europe, some from countries such as Austria, France, Germany, the Netherlands and Switzerland but the majority from Italy, Latvia, Lithuania, Poland, the Ukraine and Yugoslavia. The postwar period also saw the resumption of large-scale immigration from Ireland. From 1946 to 1959 a total of 352 000 Irish immigrants arrived in Britain. Throughout the 1950s, indeed, the Irish comprised the largest single immigrant group and levels of migration from Ireland to the British mainland reached heights not attained since the 1870s and 1880s. In the 1970s the growing prosperity of the Irish economy temporarily reduced the influx and for a time Ireland even gained on balance of migration with the mainland. By the 1980s, however, the volume of Irish immigration once more increased and the traditional net inflow of Irish to mainland Britain reasserted itself.[20]

Although relatively high levels of immigration in the 1950s and early 1960s owed much to growing numbers of coloured immigrants from the West Indies and the Indian sub-continent, they also owed a good deal to increasing levels of white immigration from countries outside the Caribbean, the New Commonwealth and Pakistan. Even excluding immigrants from the Irish Republic, as early as 1966 only 12 per cent of all United Kingdom immigrants came from Bangladesh, India, Pakistan and Sri Lanka and fewer than 7 per cent from the Caribbean. By comparison, over 16 per cent came from Australia, Canada and New Zealand, 16 per cent from other Commonwealth countries and more than 35 per cent from elsewhere. Twenty years later the respective shares of the Indian sub-continent and the Caribbean had fallen to around 10 per cent and 2 per cent, of Australia, Canada and New Zealand to 12 per cent and of other Commonwealth countries to below 12 per cent, while that of other parts of the world had risen to 58 per cent.[21] Between 1980 and 1990 immigrants

31

from the New Commonwealth and Pakistan, which by this stage provided the bulk of coloured immigration, accounted for little more than a quarter of all migrants to the United Kingdom. Almost three-quarters were drawn from countries of predominantly white settlement – 15 per cent in the Old Commonwealth, 23 per cent in the European Union and 35 per cent in other parts of the world.[22] Much of the modest decline in levels of immigration during the 1970s and early 1980s stemmed from a drop in immigration from Australia, Canada and New Zealand while much of the increase in immigration during the second half of the 1980s came from European Union and white Commonwealth countries. By the late 1980s non-Commonwealth and particularly European countries had become the main sources of immigrant flows.[23]

Immigration to the United Kingdom persisted throughout the twentieth century despite increasingly stringent legislative attempts to restrict it. Apart from temporary restrictions imposed during the French Revolutionary and Napoleonic Wars and the 'French scare' of 1848–50 no attempt was made to curb immigration until the Aliens Act of 1905, an essentially racist measure designed to reduce the influx of poor Jews from Russia and Eastern Europe in response to native working-class resentment over rising unemployment and housing shortages in the East End of London where most of these immigrants had settled. Under the provisions of the Aliens Acts of 1914 and 1919, which remained in force until 1971, similar legislation was extended to all aliens. From 1920 onwards the immigration authorities were empowered to exclude all foreign nationals who had either not received official permission to enter the country or who lacked a completed landing and embarkation card. In practice this legislation was aimed primarily at undesirables like criminals, transient seamen, political dissidents and the diseased. These apart, very few of those who wished to settle in the United Kingdom were excluded. As yet, moreover, none of this legislation applied to British or Commonwealth citizens.[24]

For many Commonwealth citizens, however, the situation changed radically in 1962. Even before the Commonwealth

Immigrants' Act of that year restrictions on the issue of passports to uneducated or unskilled persons other than those who were dependants of existing immigrants had begun to impede immigration from a number of Commonwealth countries. Prompted in part by mounting concern over unemployment but mainly by worsening racial problems, with effect from July 1962 immigration was restricted solely to dependants of immigrants already resident in the United Kingdom and to people (and their dependants) in receipt of work permits for which, for the first time, Commonwealth citizens were required to apply in the same way as foreign nationals.

Difficulties in verifying dependent status, especially for applicants from the Indian sub-continent, together with the growth of Asian immigration from newly independent East African countries, led to the imposition of still more stringent immigration controls in subsequent years. Under the terms of the 1968 Commonwealth Immigrants' Act entry was limited to United Kingdom passport holders who had either themselves been born in the United Kingdom or whose parents or grandparents either lived in the United Kingdom or were naturalised and registered as United Kingdom citizens. For those failing to meet these criteria entry was controlled by a system of vouchers which, on the whole, were available only to applicants with special skills or professional qualifications. In 1969 an Immigrants' Appeals Act required dependants from the Indian sub-continent to justify their claim for unrestricted entry before leaving home. The 1971 Immigration Act, effective from January 1973, instituted a new category of immigrant – the patrial, which effectively restricted rights to United Kingdom citizenship, and therefore to free entry, to those with parents or grandparents of British origin.[25] Although in theory unrestricted immigration was also available to families and dependants of non-patrials already resident in the United Kingdom, in these cases it was not automatic and in practice was severely limited by requirements that were difficult to understand and often impossible to satisfy.

Further restrictive legislation, aimed specifically at curbing the immigration of Commonwealth non-whites, was passed in the 1980s. In 1981 a British Nationality Act established three categories of citizenship – British, British Dependent Territories and British Overseas. Only those included in the first of these were entitled to automatic entry. In 1985 and 1986, to cope with growing numbers of illegal immigrants and the practical problems involved in attempting to verify claims for access at ports of disembarkation, immigrants from Bangladesh, Ghana, India, Nigeria, Pakistan and Sri Lanka were required to obtain their visas in advance of departure. Beginning in 1988 husbands were required to prove their ability to provide the necessary financial support for immigrant dependants and, in the case of polygamous marriages, were permitted to bring over only one wife. Anticipating an influx from Hong Kong following its return to China in 1997, the 1990 British Nationality (Hong Kong) Act limited immigration from Hong Kong to 50 000 so-called 'key' workers and their dependants.[26]

With the exception of the 1905 Aliens Act which contributed significantly to the decline in Jewish immigration from Russia and Eastern Europe in the years leading up to the First World War,[27] until the Commonwealth Immigrants' Act of 1962 the impact of legislation on the flow of immigration was minimal. Thereafter its influence increased, especially for non-white immigrants from Commonwealth countries whose entry it was principally intended to restrict. Public debate of the issue of immigration controls and a growing realisation that the introduction of some form of limitation was inevitable clearly contributed to the sharp rise which occurred in immigration from Pakistan and New Commonwealth countries in the years immediately preceding the 1962 Act. Coupled with the relaxation of US immigration laws in 1965, the Act also helps to explain why in the course of the 1960s immigration from the Indian sub-continent came to dominate that from the Caribbean. Over the last several decades too there can be no doubt that levels of non-white immigration would have been higher and the trend towards non-Commonwealth and, particularly, European immigration less marked had legislative controls of the kind that were adopted not been introduced.[28]

At the same time the effect of legislation on the extent and ethnic composition of immigrant flows should not be exaggerated. Firstly, legislation was itself largely a response to the growth of racial tension and conflict in an increasingly ethnically diverse society. Secondly, variations in the scale and geographic origins of immigration were in any case chiefly the result of political or economic circumstances, the impact of which legislative controls merely modified.

Some of those who came to Britain were motivated mainly by a desire to escape political persecution: Russian Jews fleeing the repression which followed the assassination of Tsar Alexander II in 1881 and the revolution of 1905; Irish escaping the protracted campaign for independence which culminated in the Eastern Rising of 1916 and the 'troubles' preceding the establishment of the Irish Free State and whose principal alternative destination, the USA, was increasingly restricted by immigration controls; and Europeans fleeing the tyranny of Nazism in the 1930s and the turmoil that engulfed much of central Europe in the years immediately following the Second World War. More recent instances of politically motivated immigration include Hungarians in 1956, Czechoslovakians in 1968, Asians driven out of Uganda by Idi Amin in 1972–3, Chileans forced into exile following the collapse of the Allende government, Iranians fleeing militant Islam and Chinese 'boat people' from Vietnam.

In most cases, however, the decision to move to Britain was based overwhelmingly on economic considerations. Whether the push of economic deprivation at home or the pull of economic opportunity in Britain weighted most heavily in individual decisions to migrate is difficult to determine. Probably, in the period from 1945 to the mid 1960s or early 1970s the pull of the British economy predominated. Throughout the 1950s and early 1960s shortages of labour, caused by a combination of falling fertility in the prewar years and unusually high rates of economic growth, forced employers such as British Rail, London Transport and the National Health Service to actively recruit workers from the populations of the Caribbean islands. The result was that within the period 1955–74 variations in levels of West Indian immigration correlated closely and positively with variations in levels of British employment opportunities.[29] The fact that most non-white immigrants settled in the inner zones of conurbations, where losses of population had been heaviest, and in areas like the South East, the Midlands, the West Riding and those parts of the North West which had failed to retain adequate supplies of indigenous labour rather than in areas of higher unemployment like Scotland, Wales, Merseyside and the North may be taken as further indication of the primacy of pull factors.[30]

After the mid 1960s the push of economic hardship at home began to play an increasingly important role in determining levels of immigration from Commonwealth countries. As demonstrated by the existence of a negative correlation between levels of emigration and national income on each West Indian island during the early 1960s, even Caribbean immigration had always owed something to the push of overpopulation, unemployment and poverty. In the case of immigrants from the Indian sub-continent push factors had probably always predominated over pull. Levels of immigration from the Indian sub-continent and other parts of Asia have never correlated as closely with fluctuations in British employment levels as those from the Caribbean. Even before the mid 1960s immigration from India and Pakistan owed more to the push of unemployment and land hunger at home than to the lure of opportunities for work in the United Kingdom. By the late 1970s, if not earlier, push factors dominated pull factors in the economic motives for non-white immigration from all parts of the world.[31] While the persistence of a negative relationship between United Kingdom unemployment rates and numbers of work permits issued to aliens during the period 1969–87 confirms that pull factors continued to have some influence on immigration decisions, [32] these factors were probably of greater relevance to white immigrants from non-Commonwealth and European countries than to non-white immigrants from the Commonwealth and elsewhere in the world who responded largely to push forces. Given the more or less continuous rise in British unemployment levels since the mid 1960s and the coincidence between the mid 1970s and mid 1980s of severe economic recession and the arrival onto the labour market of the children of the 1960s 'baby boom', it is not surprising that the significance of pull relative to push impulses in migration to Britain has decreased in recent years.

In the final analysis, immigration was part of a world-wide process involving a transfer of people from countries where economic opportunities were few to countries where they were more abundant. It was one of the legacies of its Empire and of the unusually high dependence of its economy on international trade and investment that Britain was more prone to immigration from a wider mix of races and countries than most.

In spite of its attractiveness to immigrants mainland Britain and each of its constituent countries have invariably lost more people to emigration than they have gained by immigration. In the case of England net migration has been more or less continuously unfavourable since at least the middle of the sixteenth century.[33] Losses on balance of migration for England and Wales since the late nineteenth century were especially severe in the 1880s, 1900s and 1910s and more moderate in the 1870s, 1890s, 1920s, 1960s and 1970s (Table 2.5). Only during the periods 1931–65 and 1981–91 was the balance of migration positive. Scotland has been even more disadvantaged by migration than England and Wales, losing more people to emigration than it gained through immigration in every decade from the 1860s to the 1980s.[34]

Possibly the most surprising feature of British migration history in the twentieth century has been the re-emergence of substantial net losses on international migration in the later 1960s, 1970s and early 1980s. At various times between the 1950s and 1970s, by contrast, other European countries began to experience either net gains or steadily diminishing net losses on balance of migration.[35] In Britain, the occasional year apart, the phenomenon of large-scale net out-migration persisted until the mid 1980s.

Underlying the vast net exodus of people from mainland Britain in the decades prior to the First World War was a

Table 2.5 Net gain or loss (–) by migration. England/Wales and
Scotland, 1871/81–1981/91 (thousands[*])

	England/Wales	Scotland
1871–81	–164	–93
1881–91	–601	–218
1891–1901	–69	–53
1901–11	–501	–254
1911–21	–620	–239
1921–31	–170	–390
1931–51	757	220
1951–61	406	–282
1961–71	–106	–327
1971–81	–149	–151
1981–91	385	–103

[*] For both England/Wales and Scotland the figures relate to migration to
and from all other destinations.

Sources: Registrar-General England and Wales, *Statistical Review for 1971.
Part II. Tables. Population* (London, 1973), p. 89. OPCS, *Population
Trends, Spring 1981* (London, 1981), p. 35. OPCS, *International
Migration 1981. United Kingdom, England and Wales* (London,
1982), p. 2. Registrar-General Scotland, *Annual Report 1990*
(Edinburgh, 1991), p. 107. OPCS, *International Migration 1991.
United Kingdom. England and Wales* (London, 1993), pp. 1–2.

unique mix of demographic, economic and technological circumstances which, facilitated by improved methods of transport and communication and a growing awareness of
conditions and opportunities overseas, combined to enhance
the attractions of the New World relative to the Old. Mass
emigration in this period, it should be stressed, was not the
consequence of an absolute decline in the capacity of the
British economy to generate opportunities for capital and
labour. On the contrary, more opportunities for wealth-
creation and work were available in late nineteenth- and early
twentieth-century Britain than ever before. Had this not been
so levels of emigration would undoubtedly have been higher.
By transforming existing economic and social systems and dis-
rupting traditional mentalities and ways of life economic development, at least in the short term, increases rather than

decreases the impetus for migration. It is therefore no coincidence that variations in the onset of mass emigration from one country to another correlated closely with the date at which modern industrialisation began nor that Britain, the most developed economy, provided the largest number of emigrants to the New World.[36] Economic growth also ensures that potential emigrants have the financial resources necessary to meet the costs of emigration. Accordingly the majority of emigrants came not from areas of greatest economic backwardness and poverty but from areas most affected by the forces of economic development and change.[37] Typically it was not the very poorest who emigrated. On the whole emigration did not serve as a safety-valve for the destitute. Most British emigrants before 1914 were people seeking to transfer from at least a minimally adequate standard of life to what they hoped would be a better standard of life overseas. Whatever may have been the case at certain times and places elsewhere in Europe, the bulk of emigrants from late nineteenth- and early twentieth-century Britain were prompted more by a desire for advancement or a wish to avoid possible, *future* destitution than by a need to escape the immediate realities of pauperism.[38]

In addition to capital an ability to emigrate requires the fulfilment of two other conditions: firstly that there is somewhere with the necessary opportunities for personal improvement to which would-be emigrants can go: secondly that potential emigrants have knowledge of these opportunities and access to a transport system capable of bringing them speedily and cheaply within reach.

Down to the middle of the nineteenth century, for the majority of people, realistic alternatives to life in Europe were extremely limited. Not until the later decades of the century were the economies of New World countries sufficiently developed to allow them to assimilate an influx of immigrants on a mass scale, and methods of transport and communication capable of transmitting large numbers of people to the new opportunities overseas. To some extent, of course, improvements in the technology of transport and communications were themselves a consequence of the growth of intercontinental passenger and freight traffic. But, by increasing the safety and reducing the opportunity-cost of travel, they also acted as powerful stimuli to emigration in their own right.[39]

In accounting for mass emigration from Europe in the decades prior to the First World War and, in particular, for the marked regional variations in its extent, the role of information diffusion and the factors influencing it deserve special emphasis. One of the more instructive aspects of late nineteenth-century county by county variations in levels of English emigration is how little they were related to variations in the extent of urbanisation, the size and structure of populations, rates of fertility, distances from the main emigration ports, levels of income among the unskilled, rates of literacy or proportions of the workforce employed in agriculture. They were, however, closely and directly related to variations in the extent of previous emigration flows. Once established, it seems, emigration built up a self-sustaining momentum, a momentum which often persisted irrespective of changes in the economic circumstances of sending or receiving countries. Ties of kinship and community initiated by earlier emigrants, together with the financial assistance these gave to those who followed, considerably reduced the emotional and monetary costs of emigration and helped perpetuate movement even when the immediate material motives for relocation were less urgent than they had previously been. Supported by the promotional activities of overseas governments, railway and steamship companies, and by the work of the Emigrants' Information Office and the numerous, voluntary emigration societies, the information contained in letters from previous emigrants and in newspaper reports of their circumstances and achievements provided a vital, additional stimulus to continued movement overseas and the directions it took. Areas where the feedback of information was greatest were precisely those areas which became emigration-saturated soonest.[40]

Clearly, the wealth generated by economic growth coupled with innovations in transport and communications and an increased awareness of the opportunities emigration afforded were important, permissive agents in the mass exodus of people from Britain and other European countries to the countries of the New World in the decades before 1914. But they were not its fundamental cause. However easy it became to go, the fact is that people would not have left had they not had good reason for doing so. At root, the phenomenon of late nineteenth- and early twentieth-century mass overseas emigration was the result of the creation of an integrated international economic system in which regions with differing rates of natural increase and differing endowments of labour, capital and raw material resources grew at different rates and in different ways. Inevitably this created both a necessity and an opportunity for labour to seek out those regions where its efforts would yield the greatest individual and aggregative return. In countries like Britain, where the increase in the size of the labour supply caused by falling mortality more closely approximated to, and at times even exceeded, the requirements of the economy for labour, expectations of continued material advance could easily be seen to be under threat. In the New World, where demand for labour generally exceeded supply, such expectations seemed more likely to be met. Mass emigration was a response to circumstances new to the late nineteenth- and early twentieth-century world when what were considered inadequate or inadequately rewarded opportunities for labour at home coincided with more favourable opportunities for labour overseas. In the absence of sufficiently rigorous and extensive controls over fertility, and wherever domestic cultural, political and social arrangements permitted, emigration was an inevitable reaction to what, for large sections of the population, were unique differentials in employment and income levels between the Old World and the New.[41]

The reappearance of large-scale emigration and of a substantial loss on balance of overseas migration after the hiatus imposed on international mobility by the First World War suggests that the disparities of opportunity between the Old World and the New continued into the 1920s. Compared with the economies of New World countries, the British economy performed poorly throughout much of the immediate postwar decade. Wage restrictions and high unemployment, especially in the export industries, made emigration an attractive proposition. For the first time since the early nineteenth century the coincidence of labour surplus at home and labour shortage in the colonies and dominions with a desire to strengthen Empire and Commonwealth ties by increasing the number of British-born settlers persuaded British governments to introduce state-funded emigration schemes.

State financial support for emigration originated in the recommendations of the Dominions' Royal Commission published in 1917. In the interests of imperial economic and political unity the Commission urged that labour (and capital) should be redistributed from the United Kingdom, where it was underemployed, poorly rewarded and therefore a potential source of social disturbance, to countries like Australia, Canada and New Zealand, where it would reduce labour and thus production costs, increase the supply of cheap food and raw materials for the mother country and enhance the ability of consumers to buy British goods. In an era of widespread tariff protection and severe depression in international trade such recommendations appeared to make a great deal of sense.

The first tentative steps towards a programme of state-sponsored emigration were taken in 1919 when free passages to the Dominions were offered to ex-servicemen and their families. The scheme accounted for almost a fifth of all emigration from Britain to Commonwealth countries between 1919 and 1927. Its success helped to pave the way for the Empire Settlement Act of 1922. This Act, which remained in force until 1937, empowered British and Dominion governments to contribute to the passage costs of any migrant nominated by friends or relatives already resident in the Dominions or prepared to work in agriculture or domestic service on arrival. At £15 a head, of which the British government could provide no more than half up to a maximum outlay of £3 million in any one year, assisted passage money represented a significant proportion of the ordinary third-class steerage fare to Australia and New Zealand (£36–£40) and especially to Canada (£18) and must have been a considerable inducement to emigrate for unskilled workers whose annual earnings averaged around £70. Little wonder that between 1922 and 1931 more than £6 million was spent on assisting 400 500 people overseas.

In addition the Empire Settlement Act permitted the imperial authorities to share interest payments on loans raised on the London money market by the Australian government for the purposes of land settlement and development. In 1925 the amount that could be borrowed was increased to £34 million and the activities on which it could be spent were widened to embrace any public work likely to increase Australia's ability to absorb immigrants. Under the provisions of the scheme British governments were required to contribute £130 000 for every £750 000 advanced by the Australian federal government to state governments. It was anticipated that the 1925 agreement would assist the emigration of around 450 000 people in the course of the following ten years. In the event, despite an expenditure in excess of £7 million on the various immigrant-absorption schemes, between 1925 and 1932 the annual total averaged barely half the expected number. Even so, over one-third of all British emigrants to Canada and nearly two-thirds of those to Australia in the period 1923–9 received some financial assistance from the state.

Empirical analysis of the relative importance of push and pull factors on emigration from the United Kingdom in the 1920s indicates that, on balance, conditions in countries of destination exerted a greater influence than conditions at home. Variations in United Kingdom income levels had no noticeable effect on levels of emigration while variations in United Kingdom unemployment rates, though closely related to fluctuations in the volume of emigration to Australia, bore no obvious relationship to those in the number of emigrants to Canada or the USA. On the other hand levels of emigration from the United Kingdom to Canada and the USA did correlate closely with variations in the *differential* between United Kingdom and Canada/USA per capita incomes. There was also a close relationship between levels of unemployment in Australia and Canada and levels of immigration from the United Kingdom.

In view of the availability of state assistance for emigration to Commonwealth destinations and the extent of the dichotomy between the performance of the British and New World economies, it is surprising that levels of emigration in the 1920s were not higher than they were. If the Australian case is typical, this cannot be explained by the effect of high wartime mortality on the number of young adult males, a reduction in the supply of agricultural workers and domestic servants or, at least until the last years of the decade, any narrowing in income differentials between Britain and the New World. A more likely explanation was the rise which occurred in the real cost of emigration. In turn this was due to a combination of higher transport costs, a relative increase in the real cost of living in countries like Australia, rising unemployment in Britain, which increased the desire for emigration but decreased the ability to finance it, and rising unemployment in Commonwealth countries, which raised the costs faced by emigrants in finding a job and at the same time prevented governments from spending more on subsidising immigration.[42]

The problems confronting would-be emigrants from the United Kingdom in the 1920s were compounded by the introduction in many of the more important countries of destination of legislation to reduce immigration.[43] True, the restrictions imposed by the various quota acts were much less serious for Britain than they were for many other emigrant-sending countries. At no time during the interwar period did the number of British emigrants to restricted destinations reach the quotas allowed. It is possible, however, that the existence of quotas worked psychologically to deter some who might otherwise have gone. The increase in emigration in 1923, partly motivated by a desire to anticipate the USA Immigration Restriction Act of 1924, may be one indication of this.[44]

Even without the introduction of legislative restrictions the relationship between in- and out-migration would have altered radically in the 1930s. In part the sharp decline in levels of emigration and the emergence of a favourable balance on international migration was a result of modest improvements

44

in employment prospects at home. In the main, however, it reflected the world-wide nature of the economic depression which occurred around 1930 and in the course of which the demand of primary-producing countries for additional labour collapsed and differentials in opportunities for labour between the Old World and the New largely disappeared.[45] In the case of the United Kingdom, where the severity of economic depression in the early 1930s was relatively muted and recovery began relatively early, these differentials disappeared almost entirely and, as a result, losses on balance of migration gave way to gains.

As noted above, in contrast to the experience of other western European countries, in Britain net losses on migration reasserted themselves in the decades following the Second World War and persisted more or less without interruption until the second half of the 1980s. The explanation lies in the performance of the economy. Measured against their own historical record, in the 25 years or so after 1945 rates of economic growth and advances in average standards of living in Britain were greater, and rates of unemployment lower, than in any previous period of comparable length. These were the circumstances chiefly responsible for the vast influx of migrants from the Caribbean and Indian sub-continent in the 1950s and 1960s. On the face of it the same circumstances might be expected to have discouraged emigration. That they did not stemmed from the fact that levels of output and standards of life rose less rapidly in Britain than almost anywhere else in the developed world. This had two consequences. First it meant that emigrants from less advanced parts of eastern and southern Europe would be more inclined to prefer countries in northern and western Europe to Britain: second that differentials in opportunity between the British economy and the economies of other developed countries, particularly those in the New World, once again became sufficiently pronounced to make emigration worthwhile. In the cases of Australia, Southern Rhodesia and New Zealand the effect of the latter was augmented by the introduction in 1953 of an Overseas Migration Board offering assisted passages of £10 a head in an effort to reinforce Commonwealth unity by increasing the share of its population that was of British descent.[46] Rising levels of unemployment from the mid 1960s and the onset of severe economic recession between the late 1970s and mid 1980s helped sustain the net loss on migration. Only with the modest recovery in rates of economic growth which occurred in the second half of the 1980s was a favourable balance on international migration restored. On the whole, however, the 1930s and latter half of the 1980s were the only peacetime periods since at least the middle of the sixteenth century to boast an economy whose attractions relative to some other economies were sufficient to ensure an excess of immigrants over emigrants.

Internal Migration

Before the middle of the nineteenth century movements of people from one county of England to another were dominated by the pull of London and high levels of mobility between a group of industrialising counties in the North and Midlands – Cheshire and Lancashire, Lancashire and Yorkshire, Staffordshire and Warwickshire. As yet there was no sign of a net south to north migrational flow nor of any marked change in a long-established pattern of movement in which people ebbed and flowed between areas with few predominant directional foci.

In the half century preceding the outbreak of the First World War geographically diffuse patterns of mobility were replaced by a tendency for migrants to gravitate towards a relatively small number of regions: in Scotland towards the Western Lowlands: in England and Wales towards London and the Home Counties, the East and West Midlands, the North West, North East and South Wales. Between 1851 and 1911 no more than one in four of all registration districts in England and Wales gained on balance of migration and no more than one in ten, the majority located in the South East, the North West and Yorkshire, did so in each decade. Almost three-quarters of all registration districts recorded net migrational losses. Especially heavy flows of emigrants went from rural areas in central, western and south-western parts of England to Glamorgan and Monmouth, from rural areas in eastern, southern and south-western England to London and the Home Counties, from everywhere in rural England to the county of Durham and, most noticeably of all, from rural to urban communities. The process, graphically described by Lawton as migration from periphery to core, peaked in the third quarter of the century. Thereafter, as the direction of migration began to shift in favour of the South East and to a lesser extent the West and East Midlands chiefly at the expense of northern industrial and coalmining regions, it slowed.[47]

Underlying these changing patterns of migration were regional disparities in the nature and pace of economic growth and thus in income levels and employment opportunities. For as long as manufacturing remained a small-scale, spatially scattered activity, agriculture the dominant occupation and urban settlements primarily service or market centres, the pattern of mobility remained circular, diffuse and short-distance. As manufacturing enterprises grew in scale and came to concentrate in fewer locations so the geography of mobility altered. Average migrant distances increased and both the direction of migrant flows and the process of urbanisation began to focus on London and the Home Counties, where the attractions of industry were aggregated by London's status as the capital and principal commercial centre, and on the rapidly industrialising regions of the North West and West Riding of Yorkshire (textiles), the North East (chemicals, coal, engineering and shipbuilding), the West Midlands (coal, copper, engineering and pottery), West Scotland (coal and iron-ore, steel, engineering, shipbuilding and textiles) and South Wales (coal, iron and steel). Outside the main industrial areas only resort, port and naval districts attracted immigrants and expanded their urban populations on a similar scale. When, in the course of the later nineteenth and early twentieth centuries, rates of economic growth in some of the

47

older mining and manufacturing districts started to decline the direction of migration slowly shifted towards the more prosperous industrial and commercial parts of the South East and Midlands.[48]

During the 1920s and 1930s, with the further decline of agriculture as an employer of labour, the more remote, rural areas of Britain, in most cases more severely than before the First World War, continued to lose large numbers of people on balance of migration with more central, urbanised locations. There were, however, some significant changes in the direction of movement. Firstly, as the pace of suburbanisation accelerated, rural areas in the vicinity of London and the larger provincial cities and towns began to gain on the ebb and flow of migration. Secondly, the tendency of Inner London to lose on net migration, already apparent in the prewar decade, intensified. Thirdly, the net exodus of people from the older industrial regions of the English North East and North West, Yorkshire, Clydeside and South Wales to Greater London and the English Midlands and, generally, from north to south Britain greatly increased.[49] The causes of this lie in the sharply contrasting regional experiences of economic growth. In those parts of the country where economies were dominated by the depressed staple industries of coal, iron and steel, cotton textiles, shipping and shipbuilding, levels of prosperity were low and rates of unemployment high. In the South East and those parts of the Midlands where service activities and the 'newer' industries of electrical engineering, chemicals and motor vehicles were most heavily concentrated, levels of prosperity and employment opportunities were greater and rates of unemployment relatively low. Inevitably, as the share of the nation's employment and wealth-generating capacity gravitated towards the southern half of the country so too did more of its people.[50]

Throughout the 1950s and 1960s levels of interregional migration increased steadily and remained high until the mid 1970s. Between the mid 1970s and mid 1980s, in line with the experience of other developed countries, they fell. Between 1985 and 1988 they once more began to rise and, despite falling in 1989, remained higher than at any time since the start of the decade.[51]

Accompanying these variations in the frequency of interregional mobility were further changes in its direction. During the 1950s and 1960s, though more obviously in the former than the latter, prewar tendencies for migrants to move from north to south and from urban to more rural regions intensified. Migrational gains were greatest in the English South East and West Midlands and migrational losses heaviest in the older industrial and mining areas of the North, North West, Yorkshire/Humberside and South Wales and, with some exceptions, in the rural peripheries of northern England, southern Scotland, parts of the Scottish Grampians and southern and western Wales. But although the relationship between settlement size and the extent and direction of migrational balance remained generally positive (smaller settlements losing and larger settlements gaining on migration), the strength of the correlation was already weakening. Positive balances on migration were now being recorded in some of the small settlements in the remoter, rural peripheries of Scotland, Wales, East Anglia, the East Midlands, the North and the South West as well as in many of those surrounding the largest urban centres. Increasingly the trend of mobility was away from the largest cities and towns towards smaller urban and rural communities. By 1966–71 all non-metropolitan regions were experiencing migrational gains and all metropolitan regions with the exception of South Yorkshire migrational losses. Within metropolitan regions movements of people were increasingly favouring less urbanised districts at the expense of the more densely populated urban cores.

The drift of people from north to south temporarily halted in the early 1970s but speeded up again after 1973 when modest net gains on migration in much of Scotland, northern and north-western England, Yorkshire/Humberside and the western Midlands once more gave way to modest but growing deficits. Throughout the 1970s and 1980s the only English regions to gain consistently on balance of migration were East Anglia, the East Midlands and, until the end of the 1980s, all parts of the South East lying outside the Greater London area. Except for Greater London where migrational balances were always unfavourable, regions of persistent net migrational loss were concentrated in the northern half of the country – in the North, North West, the West Midlands and, before the late 1980s, Yorkshire/Humberside.[52]

Over the last twenty years or so heavy net losses on migration have persisted in all the main conurbations – Greater London, Greater Manchester, Merseyside, the West Midlands, Strathclyde and Tyne and Wear. Generally the larger cities and towns of England and Wales continued to lose population to smaller urban and rural communities. In Scotland net migrational losses in the most heavily urbanised regions of the Lothians and Strathclyde contrasted sharply with net migrational gains in almost all other regions.[53] Throughout mainland Britain net losses on migration in Inner and Outer London, the principal cities of other metropolitan regions and cities within non-metropolitan regions were countered by net migrational gains in New Towns, resort, retirement and other urban communities and among rural populations. The rate at which migrants flowed from north to south and away from the main urban-industrial centres slackened after the mid 1970s, hence the deceleration in the twin processes of decentralisation and counterurbanisation.[54] But it has not yet ceased entirely.

Considerable scholarly energy has been expended in attempting to explain why in the course of the second half of the twentieth century migrational balances shifted in favour of southern and less urbanised, more peripheral parts of the country and why in the final quarter of the century the pace of decentralisation and counterurbanisation slowed down.

The north to south drift of migration which effectively began in the interwar period and which, with temporary abatements in the years immediately following the Second World War and again in the early 1970s, has continued ever since, was the consequence of fundamental changes in the structure of the economy away from mining and manufacturing towards service activities and, within the mining and manufacturing sector, away from older towards newer industries.

The trend away from mining and manufacturing towards service occupations was already well underway by the interwar decades. Between 1920–1 and 1937–8 the number of United Kingdom workers employed in mining and quarrying fell by 413 000 and in manufacturing by 129 000. Employment in the distributive trades, insurance and banking, on the other hand, rose by 770 000, in other professional and miscellaneous services by 959 000, in building, contracting, transport and communications by 319 000 and in gas, water and electricity by 106 000. Beginning in the 1970s the pace of 'deindustrialisation' accelerated. After rising by 5 per cent in the 1950s and falling by a modest 4 per cent in the 1960s, total employment in British manufacturing industry decreased by almost a quarter in the 1970s and a further quarter between 1981 and 1988. By contrast, employment in public and private sector service activities rose by 7–8 per cent between 1971 and 1981 and by around 7 per cent between 1981 and 1988. Although similar trends also occurred in other advanced economies, nowhere did they proceed as far or as fast as in Britain where weaknesses in the competitiveness of manufacturing industry and the presence of an already relatively extensive service sector gave them an extra fillip.[55]

Accompanying the shift from manufacturing to service activities were changes in the relative prosperity of different industries within the manufacturing sector. While industries like coalmining, cotton textiles, iron and steel, mechanical engineering, shipping, shipbuilding and, since the 1970s, motor vehicles have performed poorly, industries like chemicals, electricals and electronics, man-made fibres and North Sea gas and oil have done much better. It is to regional variations in the composition of industrial activity as well as in the ratio of manufacturing to service occupations that we must also turn for an explanation of the geography of recent migration. In the southern half of Britain, where service activities and the more prosperous types of manufacturing were most heavily concentrated, employment opportunities generally increasing and unemployment rates lowest, conditions favoured a net influx of migrants. In northern Britain, except in the north of Scotland where employment opportunities were boosted by the development of the offshore oil industry, and Wales, employment levels fell, rates of unemployment were higher and the average length of time spent unemployed longer.[56] The result was a net outflow of migrants.

Variations in the relative prosperity of the manufacturing and service sectors and of different industries within the manufacturing sector also largely explain why the net flow of people southwards was less pronounced in the late 1940s, 1960s and early 1970s than in the 1950s and after the mid 1970s.

In the years immediately following the Second World War levels of net emigration from northern Britain were substantially reduced by the beneficial effects of postwar economic reconstruction programmes on the prosperity of the region's iron and steel, engineering, shipbuilding, coalmining and textile industries. By the 1950s, when most of the more urgent needs of reconstruction had been met and other economies had sufficiently recovered from the devastation of war to re-emerge as serious competitors to Britain in export markets, the prosperity of the north's staple industries diminished and rates of net out-migration accordingly rose. Aided by a moderate increase in manufacturing activity and a resurgence in the fortunes of the mining industry due to the oil crisis of the early 1970s, the temporary decline in levels of net emigration from north to south during the 1960s and early 1970s owed much to the introduction of government policies specifically designed to restrict the growth of employment in the more prosperous south and encourage investment in the relatively depressed industrial and mining regions of the north.[57] With the onset of severe economic recession in 1974 the ability of government policy to redress regional imbalances in employment opportunities effectively ceased. As Goddard points out, regional investment- and employment-generating programmes are much less likely to be effective when recession conditions are as deep and as prolonged as they were in Britain during the late 1970s and early 1980s. In part this is because severe recession decreases the supply of investable funds available for redirection; in part because as labour shortages in the more prosperous regions decline in the face of rising unemployment the incentive to divert investment towards regions of higher unemployment and greater labour surplus lessens. But the inability of regional development policy to have the same impact in the 1970s as in the 1960s also resulted from two other circumstances: first the fact that such limited investment in manufacturing as there was tended to be capital- rather than labour-intensive and was therefore, on balance, job displacing rather than job creating; and second the fact that British companies increasingly preferred to invest in newly industrialising countries overseas where, even after taking regional subsidies into account, labour and operating costs were lower than in assisted regions at home.[58] In any case, by the 1980s, partly in recognition of the failure of recent regional development policies and partly out of philosophical preference for a non-interventionist state role, Conservative governments largely abandoned the policies of the 1960s and 1970s, leaving the fate of regional economies and thus the volume and direction of migration to the ebb and flow of free market forces. Because the recession of the mid 1970s to mid 1980s was more severe in the north than the south and because recovery in the later 1980s was based chiefly on the growth of employment in the service sector, particularly that located in London and the South East, a further surge in the net flow of people southwards was inevitable.[59]

The factors responsible for the patterns of migration that underlay the postwar processes of counterurbanisation and decentralisation and for the slowing down of these processes since the early 1970s are less easy to unravel.

To some extent counterurban and decentralised patterns of migration were simply the continuance of a long-standing tendency for large urban settlements to overflow existing boundaries and spill over into an ever-widening circle of suburbanised communities in their immediate hinterlands.[60] But the importance of this factor should not be overstated. Suburbanisation was the dominant form of residential deconcentration only in the period before the late 1960s or early 1970s. Subsequently it was displaced by a genuine counterurbanisation phenomenon driven by motives much more complex than a simple desire for social segregation on which the process of suburbanisation was primarily based.[61] While it is difficult to determine the relative significance of suburban and counterurban influences on migration flows in regions bordering on urban cores, there can be no doubt that the net movement of people towards more distant, smaller urban and rural settlements, the novel feature of postwar human spatial redistribution, was motivated by factors other than mere suburban drift.

Among these factors were the forces of demographic change. Just as overpopulation and a lack of employment in rural areas had fuelled migration to urban areas in the nineteenth century, so by the middle of the twentieth century rural depopulation created conditions ripe for a reversal in the direction of net migrational flows.[62] That such a reversal occurred also owed something to the fact that by the 1950s and 1960s problems of overcrowding and housing shortage in the conurbations had become so serious that ever-growing numbers of people were compelled to find accommodation far beyond their orbit. The establishment of the New and Expanded Town programme was designed, at least in part, to reduce what were considered to be unacceptably high levels of population density in Greater London and other conurbations. It is surely significant that the period of most intense counterurban migration flow, the 1960s and early 1970s, coincided with a rise in levels of fertility to a postwar peak. Together with rising divorce rates and a growing tendency for young adults and the elderly to live separately from their families, this greatly intensified demands for additional housing space. By increasing the number of school-age and adolescent children in the household it also necessitated the construction of larger dwellings at a price that was affordable only in areas remote from the largest urban centres and their suburbs.[63]

Recent changes in the geography of net migration flows have also owed a good deal to a growing preference for life outside large urban conglomerations. Anti-urban sentiments, of course, were not unique to the postwar period nor to Britain. In all modern industrial societies, almost from the inception of mass urban living, the congestion, pollution, comparative lawlessness and stress of life in teeming urban communities have provoked a powerful reaction in favour of what was perceived to be the idyll of rural environments and their associated values. In the postwar era however, intensified from the late 1960s by a growing concern for ecological-environmental problems, dissatisfaction with urban lifestyles increased.[64] Surveys carried out in the early 1990s indicated that as many as two-thirds of all city dwellers would have preferred to live in a small town or village. Of those surveyed over half included dirt and noise among the reasons for their dissatisfaction with city life, nearly half cited the attractions of rural, open spaces and around a fifth the desire for a less stressful environment. Other, less frequently stated, concerns included overcrowding and crime, the lack of community spirit and the difficulty of bringing up children in urban areas.[65]

A preference for small town or rural residence was a particularly important stimulus to migration among the elderly and the retired who moved in growing numbers first to seaside and spa towns and from the 1970s, when property prices in established retirement areas reached prohibitive levels, increasingly to remoter, rural destinations. But it figured prominently in the motives for migration among males of all adult ages.[66] Thus data for 1983 indicate that for well over half of all non-Scottish migrants to the Highlands and Islands, whose average age was below the national average and considerably below that of the communities they joined, the search for a more pleasant environment was the prime motive for movement.[67] Clearly, for substantial numbers of people the scenic attractions, relative tranquillity, less polluted and more relaxed nature of life in rural areas were significant considerations and migrants of working age were often prepared to make considerable sacrifices of income and occupational status to satisfy them.

Since the Second World War, moreover, it has become easier for larger numbers of people than ever before to translate a desire to escape city life into reality. One reason for this was the further advances which occurred in methods of communication and transport (particularly the increase in motorway and trunkroad mileage and the extent of car ownership) which improved accessibility to large urban centres, increased the amount of information available on conditions in more distant places and facilitated contact between those who moved and the relatives and friends they left behind. Another was the improvement that occurred in the quality of the social infrastructure in rural communities (in, for example, education and health provision, electricity and water supply and standards of housing and home entertainment) which provided rural populations with many of the amenities hitherto only enjoyed by urban residents, and thus enhanced the attractiveness of rural life. A third was the growing familiarity of rural environments brought about by more leisure travel, the greater geographic mobility of employees during their working lives and an increase in the extent of second home ownership. A fourth was the decline in average ages of retirement and semi-retirement which reduced the length of time people spent tied to a specific place by their employment. But the factor which more than any other made it possible to translate residential ideals into reality was the dramatic postwar rise in levels of material affluence. In turn this was a combined result of several influences: rising real wages and the part played by technological innovation in increasing the share of the workforce employed in better-paid, non-manual occupations; higher state social security payments and a growth in the number of private occupational pension schemes; and the substantial rise in house prices, particularly in South East England.[68] Together these provided the levels of income and saving necessary to permit more of those disillusioned with city life to move to smaller urban and rural settlements. It is no coincidence that when, in the 1960s and early 1970s, the growth of affluence was most rapid, the processes of counterurbanisation and decentralisation were at their peak.

Probably the most important single cause of the tendency for net migration balances in the postwar period to shift in favour of less urbanised, geographically more diffuse locations was the growth of employment opportunities in the less densely populated regions of the country. Of the various factors responsible for this, special emphasis should be given to the development of the rural leisure and tourist industry, extensive investment in afforestation programmes and the support given by the European Union to British farming, the construction of nuclear power stations at sites remote from the main centres of population and, particularly in northern Scotland, the development of an offshore oil and gas industry and its ancillary activities.[69] The main cause, however, was the changes which took place in the location of manufacturing industry.

To some extent, it is true, these changes were as much a consequence as a cause of the new patterns of migration, a response to opportunities created by changes in the spatial distribution of residence that had occurred for other reasons.[70] Even so, there can be no doubt that the dispersal of manufacturing industry acted as a powerful stimulus to the emergence of counterurban, decentralised migrational flows. Beginning in the 1960s, the geography of manufacturing employment in Britain and other advanced economies increasingly shifted away from the conurbations and largest cities towards rural areas and the smaller cities and towns lying beyond the major urban populations.[71] In part this was a consequence of increasing concentration of ownership and control in industry; in part a consequence of an equalisation of production conditions caused by wider access to more standardised transport and communications networks, health and education services and public utilities; and in part the result of changes in technology which not only deskilled many jobs, thereby facilitating the employment of untrained labour, but also reduced the necessity for goods to be produced only in areas where they could be serviced by large workforces based on a single workplace.[72] Fielding argues that the new patterns of migration which underlay the processes of counterurbanisation and decentralisation can best be understood as a product of the transformation from an economy in which each place was involved in all aspects of the production of the goods it manufactured, to one in which each place came to specialise in particular aspects of the production function. Until the 1960s the former was the dominant characteristic, hence the net influx of people to urban areas. From the 1960s the latter has become more and more common. Increasingly the major cities came to focus on management activities and activities closely related to management decisions – marketing, banking, insurance and other financial services, taxation and other forms of legal advice. Prestige environments within easy reach of the major cities focused on research and development while smaller cities and towns and rural areas remote from the metropolitan cores and the older industrial centres took over the task of manufacturing.[73] The effect was an adjustment of net migration flows in favour of less heavily populated and more peripheral regions where the growth of employment was greatest.

The explanation for the emergence of this new spatial distribution of manufacturing is complex. Partly it was a consequence of the growing share of output taken by large national and multinational, multiplant organisations which lacked long-standing ties with particular communities and which were better able than smaller organisations both to recognise the advantages of spatially disaggregated production and to introduce it. Partly it reflected the emergence of high-tech industries which, because they required relatively small workforces, did not need to locate near to large labour markets and could therefore pay more attention to residential preferences in their location decisions. And partly it stemmed from the fact that the growth rate of new companies is greater in small towns because smaller businesses are more inclined to establish themselves in areas where the existing size of firm is small than in areas where it is large. Above all, however, it reflected the cost advantages that accrued from siting industry in areas where space was plentiful and therefore cheap, where an abundance of female or non-unionised labour kept labour costs down, and where labour relations were relatively good and, as a result, the productivity of labour likely to be higher. To varying degrees cost considerations of this kind were applicable to all advanced economies. In Britain, however, the comparatively poor performance of industry in terms of sales, profitability and general competitiveness rendered them especially crucial.[74]

In the period between the 1950s and early 1970s changes in the location of industry also owed something to the implementation of regional economic policies designed to combat problems of overpopulation and social deprivation in the inner cities and encourage the development of new or expanded towns in less heavily populated areas, and particularly in areas where older industries were in decay and employment opportunities too limited to prevent large-scale net out-migration. Though their influence should not be overstated, state-supported inner city slum clearance initiatives, coupled with the introduction of planning restrictions on suburban housing development and active programmes for the creation of new towns and the relocation of small industries to rural areas, certainly contributed to the new patterns of migration which underlay the particularly rapid rate of counterurbanisation and decentralisation characteristic of the period.[75]

Amendments to state regional economic policy also help to explain why the pace of counterurbanisation and decentralisation subsequently slowed down. By the mid 1970s policy preferences had changed in favour of inner city rejuvenation. The emphasis of inner city housing programmes switched from slum clearance, road construction and the replacement of housing by offices to the preservation and improvement of the existing housing stock and the redevelopment of previously cleared land with housing suitable especially for the elderly and young single-person or single-parent families. Simultaneously public support in the form of labour subsidies and capital investment for farming, forestry and local government services in rural and semi-rural areas was reduced, the new and expanded town programme wound up and efforts to attract investment back to older urban centres intensified.[76] All this helped to diminish the flight from the cities.

The main causes of the recent deceleration in the pace of counterurbanisation and decentralisation, however, lie in a combination of demographic and economic circumstances. Negligible rates of population growth in the 1970s and population decline in the 1980s ended the need for urban overspill. Declining household size – a product of falling fertility, rising numbers of divorced and single-parent families and an increased preference for the material benefits of a dual-income, no-child lifestyle – made it easier to provide suitable accommodation in crowded urban areas. Moreover, as the baby boom cohorts of the late 1950s and early 1960s reached young adulthood, the pressures in favour of a return to the cities in search of work and social recreation intensified. At the other end of the age scale declining proportions of the elderly in the population from the 1970s lessened the need for retirement migration at precisely the time when the saturation of many traditional retirement areas increasingly limited its feasibility.[77]

To the impact of demographic change must be added that of economic recession. During the second half of the 1970s and early 1980s, in Britain as in many other economies, prolonged recession drastically curtailed opportunities for migration. Recession meant fewer job vacancies, lower rates of job turnover, less need for new industrial sites in greenfield locations and lower levels of housebuilding. Higher rates of unemployment in hitherto prosperous small town and rural environments undermined their attractiveness to potential city emigrants and encouraged disillusioned migrants to return to the cities. Except for Hatfield, Letchworth, Stevenage and Welwyn Garden City in the South East of England, which remained prosperous until the cutbacks in defence and aerospace expenditure in the early 1990s, none of the new and expanded towns were able to offer opportunities for employment on a scale sufficient to maintain net immigration at the levels prevalent in the 1960s and early 1970s. Even during the brief interval of economic recovery in the second half of the 1980s, the fact that much of the new employment that was created lay in higher level service occupations merely served to reinforce the decline which has occurred since the mid 1970s in the rate of migrational drift from the largest urban centres. The effects of this were compounded by reductions in local authority spending. Just as the growth in public sector employment generated by local government reorganisation in 1974–5 worked temporarily to prolong the processes of counterurbanisation and decentralisation, so the progressive decline in local authority expenditure under the impact of government anti-inflationary and monetarist policies in the late 1970s and 1980s worked to curb them.[78] While these factors were not sufficiently powerful to entirely halt, let alone reverse, the postwar tendency for migration to favour counterurban, decentralised patterns of residence, they have certainly been strong enough to moderate its pace.

3
MORTALITY

Trends in average annual crude death rates (deaths per thousand total population) for England/Wales and Scotland since the middle of the nineteenth century are summarised in Table 3.1. Despite making no allowance for the influence of variations in the age and sex structure of populations, the story they tell is accurate enough for most purposes.

In both England/Wales and Scotland a substantial and generally continuous decline in mortality began around 1870 and accelerated during the opening decade of the twentieth century.[1] Similar early declines in mortality occurred elsewhere in Europe: in Austria, Belgium, European Russia, Germany, Hungary, Italy, the Netherlands, Poland and Switzerland also from the 1870s; in Yugoslavia from the 1880s; and in Bulgaria, Portugal, Romania and Spain from the 1890s or 1900s.[2]

In the case of England and Wales average decennial crude death rates for males and females together fell in each successive decade from 1871–80 to 1921–30 before stabilising at marginally higher levels in the 1930s and 1940s and declining sharply in the 1950s. Since then there has been little further improvement. During the 1950s and 1960s, indeed, death rates actually rose. Between the mid 1970s and mid 1980s, when slight reductions in age-specific mortality rates were

offset by the effects of a rise in the average age of the popula-
tion, crude death rates altered little one way or the other.[3]
Only towards the end of the 1980s did levels of mortality in
England and Wales once more begin to decline.

In the case of Scotland annual average decennial crude
death rates for males and females combined fell in each successive decade from the 1860s to the 1950s, remained at the
new low throughout the 1960s and then stabilised at a slightly
higher level in the 1970s and 1980s. Overall, between 1871–80
and 1981–90 crude death rates fell by 46 per cent in England
and Wales and 43 per cent in Scotland, the bulk of the decline
occurring in the last quarter of the nineteenth and first
quarter of the twentieth centuries. As in other advanced
economies, most of the further reduction in mortality since
the Second World War occurred in the 1950s.[4] Subsequent
improvements in mortality rates were relatively modest
everywhere.

Two other features of Table 3.1 deserve emphasis. Firstly,
except during the third quarter of the nineteenth century,
crude death rates have always been higher in Scotland than
England/Wales, though the difference was barely discernible
in the later decades of the nineteenth century and much
greater between 1901–10 and 1931–40 than in the second half
of the twentieth century. Secondly, mortality has always been
higher among males than females. Both in England/Wales
and Scotland, however, the differential narrowed considerably
in the course of the 1980s.

The impact of death rates on trends in average expectations
of life at birth is shown in Table 3.2. In the nineteenth century
advances in life expectancy were relatively modest and
confined mainly to the final quarter of the century.[5] The pace
of improvement quickened dramatically from around the
beginning of the twentieth century. In England and Wales life
expectation at birth for males rose from about 50 years, for
the cohort born 1900–4, to over 65 years, for the cohort born
1940–4, and an estimated 73 years for the cohort born
1988–90; for females from around 57 to over 72 and over 78
respectively. In Scotland it increased from under 45 (males)

Table 3.1 Annual average crude death rates, by sex. England/Wales and Scotland, 1838/50–1981/90

	England and Wales			Scotland		
	Male	Female	Both sexes	Male	Female	Both sexes
1838–50	23.2	21.6	22.4			
1851–60	23.1	21.4	22.2	(1855–60) 21.7	19.9	20.8
1861–70	23.7	21.4	22.5	23.1	21.2	22.1
1871–80	22.7	20.1	21.4	22.6	20.7	21.7
1881–90	20.3	18.1	19.1	19.7	18.7	19.2
1891–1900	19.3	17.2	18.2	19.0	18.0	18.5
1901–10	16.4	14.4	15.4	17.1	16.1	16.6
1911–20	16.0	13.0	14.4	16.0	14.8	15.4
1921–30	12.9	11.4	12.1	14.4	13.2	13.8
1931–40	13.1	11.5	12.3	14.1	12.7	13.4
1941–50	14.0	11.0	12.3	14.5	12.1	13.1
1951–60	12.4	10.9	11.6	12.9	11.3	12.1
1961–70	12.4	11.2	11.7	13.0	11.3	12.1
1971–80	12.3	11.4	11.9	13.0	11.8	12.3
1981–90	11.7	11.3	11.5	12.5	12.2	12.3

Sources: B. R. Mitchell, *British Historical Statistics* (Cambridge, 1988), pp. 57–9. Registrar-General Scotland, *Annual Report 1991* (Edinburgh, 1992), p. 19. OPCS, *Mortality Statistics. Area.* Series DH5, Nos. 8–17. OPCS, *Mortality Statistics 1991. Causes.* Series DH2, No. 18.

Table 3.2 Expectation of life at birth in years, by sex.
England/Wales and Scotland, *c*.1900–1988/90

England and Wales			Scotland		
Cohort born	Male	Female	Cohort born	Male	Female
1900–4	49.9	56.8	1891–1900	44.7	47.4
1905–9	53.1	59.8			
1910–14	55.7	61.9	1910–12	50.1	53.2
1915–19	58.8	65.7			
1920–4	60.1	66.8	1920–2	53.1	56.4
1925–9	61.9	68.7			
1930–4	63.4	70.3	1930–2	56.0	59.5
1935–9	64.9	71.3			
1940–4	65.4	72.3	1942–4	59.8	64.6
1950–2	66.4	71.5	1950–2	64.4	68.7
1961	68.1	74.0	1961	66.3	72.0
1971	69.0	75.2	1971	67.3	73.7
1981	71.0	77.0	1981	69.0	75.2
1988–90	73.0	78.5	1988–90	70.8	76.6

Sources: R. Schoen and J. Baj, 'Twentieth Century Cohort Marriage and
Divorce in England and Wales', *Population Studies*, 38, 3 (1984),
442. CSO, *Annual Abstract of Statistics 1961* (London, 1961),
pp. 36–7. T.Devis, 'The Expectation of Life in England and
Wales', *Population Trends*, 60 (1990), 24. CSO, *Annual Abstract
of Statistics 1993* (London, 1993), p. 42. Registrar-General
Scotland, *Annual Report 1980* (Edinburgh, 1982), p. 270.

and over 47 (females) in the 1890s birth cohort to over 64
(males) and nearly 69 (females) in the early 1950s cohort and
almost 71 (males) and over 76 (females) in the late 1980s
cohort. As in other countries, advances in longevity in Britain
have been predominantly a twentieth-century phenomenon.[6]

The relatively modest improvement in life expectancy
achieved during the late nineteenth century stemmed chiefly
from declining rates of mortality in the child, adolescent and
young adult age groups (1–44), where chances of survival were
already comparatively high around the middle decades of the
century.[7] Substantial decreases of mortality among infants
(0–1) and adults over the age of 45 did not effectively begin
until the twentieth century.[8] In the case of infant mortality,

however, the apparent discontinuity in trend around 1900 should not be overdramatised. In as many as 40 of the 55 counties and regions of Britain analysed by Lee, infant death rates peaked as early as 1861 or 1871 and, apart from a temporary increase in the 1890s, fluctuated around a steadily declining mean from then until the start of the twentieth century when a continuous decline became the norm everywhere.[9] Similar reductions in infant mortality in the decades before the First World War were recorded in most western European countries. In Belgium, France and, possibly, Italy, with a short-lived upsurge in the late 1890s, death rates in infancy fell from about 1890. In the Netherlands, Prussia and Sweden, where a temporary rise occurred in 1900, the decline began around 1880. Only in Britain was there an increase in national average levels of infant mortality between the 1880s and 1890s.[10]

Once underway the decline in infant death rates continued almost without interruption. In England and Wales levels of infant mortality fell from 154 per thousand live births in 1900 to 75 in 1925, 30 in 1950, 16 in 1975 and 8 in 1990, at least halving in each successive 25-year period. Before the First World War they were invariably higher than in Scotland. Between 1912 and 1977, by contrast, Scottish infant mortality rates exceeded those in England and Wales. Not until the late 1970s and 1980s was parity restored. Despite this generally less favourable record, in Scotland too death rates in infancy have plummeted in the twentieth century, from 128 per thousand live births in 1900 to 39 in 1950 and 8 in 1990.

Perhaps the most surprising feature of infant mortality trends in the present century has been their continued decline during the years of the two world wars and throughout the decades of severe economic depression between the wars. The decrease in infant death rates between 1914 and 1918 was unique to Britain and was especially marked in urban-industrial areas where, in the prewar period, levels of poverty, overcrowding and mortality in infancy had been greatest. Most of the improvement in infant life expectancy during and after the First World War was the result of falling death rates among infants aged between one and eleven months (post neonatal mortality). Death rates at ages up to one week (perinatal mortality) and from one to three weeks (neonatal mortality) fell more slowly.[11] At differing levels and rates, similar trends were apparent throughout Europe.

The greatest advances in life expectancy during the twentieth century have occurred in infancy (0–1) and childhood (1–4) and, to a lesser extent, among adolescents and young adults (15–24) and adults aged between 25 and 44. In each of these age groups the bulk of the improvement had been achieved by the middle years of the century. Rates of maternal mortality (defined as women dying during pregnancy or childbirth), which in England and Wales remained at around 4 per thousand live births between 1900–2 and 1936–7 and in Scotland rose from below 5 per thousand in 1900–2 to over 6 per thousand in 1930–2, had also already fallen to just 1 per thousand by the early 1950s.[12] In the age groups 45–54, 55–64 and 65–74, though mortality fell more or less continuously from the beginning of the twentieth century, most of the decline did not occur until the second half of the century. Death rates among men and women aged 80 and above did not begin to decline until the 1940s since when they have decreased slowly if erratically.[13]

Except in the case of males and females aged 15–44 during the latter half of the 1980s for whom death rates rose,[14] the only significant interruptions to the long-term decline in levels of mortality were those that occurred during the world wars. For both sexes and for all age groups above infancy death rates increased between 1914 and 1918. For obvious reasons the increase was especially pronounced among men aged between 17 and 36.[15] The impact of the Second World War on the life expectancy of civilians was less uniform and, on the whole, less detrimental. In Scotland mortality among males aged 15 and above was higher in 1940 than 1935 and for those aged 15–34 remained higher in 1945. Among females death rates between 1935 and 1940 fell in the age groups 0–1 and 15–54, changed little for those aged 1–14 and rose for those aged over 55. By 1945 death rates in all age groups of

Scotland's female population were lower than they had ever been before. In England and Wales mortality among males aged 15 and above increased between 1931–5 and 1940 while that of males under 15 either declined or remained stable. Between 1940 and 1945 civilian male death rates decreased in all age groups except 20–4. Among the civilian female population of England and Wales death rates between 1931–5 and 1940 rose for the age groups above 55 and either fell or remained unchanged for those below 55. Between 1940 and 1945 mortality declined for females of all ages.

Mortality by Region and Social Class

From the time when reasonably reliable data on rates of mortality first became available around the middle of the nineteenth century, expectations of life at birth have always varied substantially by region and socio-occupational class. In the case of the former the degree of variation has steadily diminished in more recent times. At the start of the twentieth century regional differentials in infant mortality ranged from under 100 per thousand live births in rural areas such as Dorset, Rutland, the Scottish Highlands, Westmorland and Wiltshire to between 150 and 170 per thousand in industrial and mining areas such as Durham, the East and West Ridings of Yorkshire, Lancashire, Northumberland, Nottinghamshire and South Wales. In the course of the period 1881–1921/31 regional differentials in infant death rates widened. Thereafter they gradually converged and by 1971 were less pronounced than at any time since the mid nineteenth century. Despite this the geography of regional infant mortality variation changed little throughout the first three-quarters of the twentieth century, with death rates in infancy in the southern half of England (the East, South East, South West, East and West Midlands regions), for example, remaining well below those in Wales and northern England (the North, North West and Yorkshire/Humberside regions). By the mid 1980s the regional geography of infant mortality levels in England had begun to change. Although the likelihood of surviving infancy was still lowest in the North West and highest in East Anglia, regions with relatively low infant death rates now included the North, the North East and Merseyside while the West Midlands had joined the North West as an area where the chances of surviving the perils of infancy were poorest.[16]

Regional variations in mortality in other age groups followed a broadly similar trend. Here too, though regional inequalities narrowed, the traditional ranking of regions by mortality level persisted largely unchanged. Around 1900 life expectation at birth in rural areas substantially exceeded that in non-agricultural and urban areas and was higher in commercial than in industrial or mining districts. Urban-rural inequalities in longevity, however, had already begun to decline. By 1911 a ten or eleven year advantage in the life expectancy of rural over urban dwellers had already shrunk to just three or four years.[17] By the mid 1920s differentials in life expectation in favour of agricultural over non-agricultural populations were only half those of a quarter of a century earlier. Thereafter, especially for males, they continued to decrease.[18] But they have never entirely disappeared. In Britain as elsewhere in northern and western Europe male longevity in the years 1969–77 was still lower in urban, dockyard, mining and heavy industrial areas than in suburban and agricultural districts. Albeit less noticeably, in the 1980s, as in the first decade of the century, rates of mortality increased and life expectancies decreased as one moved from South and East to North and North West England and on into Scotland and from rural to urban-industrial environments.[19]

Generally mortality has everywhere and always varied inversely with socio-occupational class. On the eve of the First World War socio-occupational differentials in death rates, though still considerable, were less extreme than at any time since at least the middle of the nineteenth century.[20] After the war, in contrast to trends in regional mortality differentials and despite the establishment of the National Health Service in 1946, variations in mortality by social class widened. In 1895–7 the lowest rates of infant mortality were found in social class

VIII (agricultural labourers). Otherwise death rates in infancy varied more or less negatively with social class, rising progressively from class I (professional occupations such as lawyers and physicians) through classes II (managerial and lower status professional occupations like teachers), III (skilled manual and clerical workers), IV (the semi-skilled), V (the unskilled), VI (textile workers) to class VII (miners). By 1910 infant mortality was lowest in social class I, followed in ascending order of severity by classes VIII, II, III, IV, V, VI and VII. On average, death rates among infants of unskilled workers were roughly twice as high as those with fathers in professional occupations. By the end of the interwar period, chiefly as a result of developments in the 1920s, class differentials in infant death rates were even more pronounced and by the 1970s and 1980s, when mortality among infants of the unskilled was at least twice as high as among those of professional people, as great as at any time since the beginning of the century.[21]

In other age groups too social class mortality differentials have widened in recent decades. Among males aged 15–64, for instance, standardised mortality ratios in social class V, where mortality was highest, exceeded those in social class I, where mortality was lowest, by 23 per cent in 1930–3, 37 per cent in 1949–53, 88 per cent in 1959–63 and 78 per cent in 1970–2. Differences in adult male standardised mortality ratios between social classes III and IV/V were likewise much greater by the early 1970s than fifty years or so earlier. In England and Wales by the beginning of the 1980s death rates at ages 1–4 were two to three times higher for social class V than social class I: at ages 5–9 about twice as high: and at ages 10–14 between one and a half and two times higher. In the course of the period 1930/2–1976/81 standardised mortality ratios for men aged 15–64 in social class V deteriorated from 11 to 24 per cent above the average for England and Wales while for those in social class I they improved from 10 to 34 per cent below the national average.[22] As these figures illustrate, in the main it has been the higher status social groups that have benefited most from the great improvement in life expectation during the twentieth century.

Between the mid nineteenth and mid twentieth centuries, when the bulk of the mortality decline occurred, falling death rates were predominantly due to the demise of communicable, infectious disease as the principal cause of death. As much as two-fifths of the decline in mortality between 1848/51 and 1971 stemmed from reductions in the incidence and fatality of airborne infections such as bronchitis, diphtheria, influenza, measles, pneumonia, scarlet fever, smallpox and, above all, respiratory tuberculosis. A further fifth was a consequence of reduced death rates from water-, insect- or foodborne infections such as cholera, diarrhoea, dysentery, typhoid and typhus. Other infections – convulsions, syphilis, puerperal fever and the like – together accounted for about one-eighth of the decline. Not more than a quarter of the dramatic improvement in life expectation between the mid nineteenth century and the early 1970s stemmed from a decline in mortality from causes of death other than viral or bacterial infections. Since death rates from infectious disease were greatest among infants, children and young adults, it is not surprising that these were the age groups to benefit most from the impressive advance in longevity that was achieved prior to the middle of the twentieth century.

By the second half of the century deaths from communicable infections had decreased to such an extent that they were replaced as the main causes of death by non-communicable, degenerative diseases such as ischaemic heart disease and cancers, the so-called 'diseases of affluence' which primarily affect the older age groups. Most of the relatively modest decline in death rates which occurred after the Second World War was due to a reduction in mortality from degenerative diseases, though mortality from the most significant of these – ischaemic heart disease and cancers of the lungs and bronchus – remained higher, and declined later, in England and Wales and particularly in Scotland, than in most other countries of the developed world.[23] Within Britain death rates from heart disease and cancers, as from many of the other main causes of death, were highest among the populations of the inner cities, the blue-collar suburbs and the industrial regions of South Wales, South West Scotland, Lancashire, Teesside and Yorkshire.[24]

In view of its importance to the unprecedented rise in human life expectancy during the late nineteenth and first half of the twentieth centuries it is surprising how little is known about the factors responsible for the decline in mortality from infectious disease. One possible explanation is that, in part at least, it was the consequence of either a natural reduction in the virulence of infectious disease organisms themselves or of a genetically-inspired rise in levels of human resistance to such organisms. Particularly through the impact they had on deaths from scarlet fever, smallpox and typhus, autonomous influences of this kind, it is suggested, may have accounted for as much as a fifth to a third of the overall decline in mortality during the second half of the nineteenth century and continued to play the major role in the further decline in mortality from streptococcal diseases such as scarlet fever, nephritis and rheumatic fever which persisted throughout the first half of the twentieth century.[25]

That forces independent of human action do have an effect on levels of mortality is clear from the events of the 1890s when a fortuitous sequence of hot, dry summers combined with the general unhealthiness of urban environments to raise death rates from diarrhoeal disease.[26] On the other hand, especially for that part of the modern mortality decline which occurred in the twentieth century, the significance of autonomous changes in the virulence of, and resistance to, disease organisms should not be overstated. Trends in the case-fatality rates of diseases like tuberculosis suggest that for most infectious diseases there was no long-term decline in virulence. Even the reduction in mortality from scarlet fever, considered the best example of a disease whose natural severity has diminished in recent times, owed something to the spread of isolation hospitals which helped to lessen the risks of transmission and reduce its fatality. While a decline in the virulence of the B-haemolytic streptococcus may have contributed to the continued decrease in maternal deaths from puerperal sepsis after the Second World War, it cannot easily account for the sudden, sharp drop in mortality from this infection which occurred around 1937.[27] As even the supporters of the autonomous interpretation acknowledge, the bulk of the explanation for the demise of infectious disease as the principal cause of death must lie somewhere within the realm of human activity. The difficulty has always been to determine which of the improvements made by man to his personal and environmental condition have contributed most to the prolongation of life.

One school of thought holds that special significance should be attached to man's success in raising his standards of nutrition, thereby increasing his resistance to infectious disease and enhancing the likelihood of recovery when infection did strike. Thus, according to McKeown and his co-authors, dietary improvement, particularly via its impact on mortality from tuberculosis and to a lesser extent typhus, probably accounted for as much as half of the increase in life expectancy between 1850 and 1900 and remained the major cause of falling death rates, especially from airborne infections such as tuberculosis and measles, throughout the first three-quarters of the twentieth century.[28] According to Winter, while other factors were *necessary*, improvements in nutrition were the only *sufficient* cause of the decline in infectious disease mortality between 1870 and 1950. Without significant advances in standards of diet, death rates from diseases such as bronchitis, influenza, pneumonia, scarlet fever, tuberculosis and whooping cough would not have declined as they did. Improved nutrition, Winter argues, was the chief reason for the continued reduction in infant death rates during the years of the First World War and one of the chief reasons for improvements in the health of mothers and babies even during the worst years of economic depression in the 1930s.[29]

Most historians, however, take a more conservative view of the contribution of nutritional improvement to mortality decline. Though none would deny that variations in diet played some part in accounting for secular, spatial and socio-occupational variations in life expectation, the role of nutrition is usually regarded, at best, as no more crucial than that of a number of other important influences or, at worst, as very much secondary to the contribution of other factors.

Even in the late nineteenth century, when its effect is likely to have been greatest, there are good reasons not to overstate the role of nutrition. That some advances in nutritional standards occurred before 1900, even among the poorest, is indisputable.[30] But for the majority of the working-class population these advances were modest, and some would say negligible.[31] The belief that working-class diets in the late nineteenth century were sufficiently superior to those of earlier times to have a significant impact on levels of resistance to infectious disease has still to be convincingly demonstrated. Furthermore, if nutritional standards were as vital as some have claimed why did females, who received a disproportionately small share of the family food supply, live longer than males, and middle-class infants, who probably consumed a disproportionately large share of less nutritious patent foods, experience lower mortality rates than working-class infants?[32] Given that improvements in diet were no greater for urban than rural populations, it is equally difficult to reconcile trends in nutrition with the fact that in the half century or so before 1914 death rates fell more quickly in urban than rural areas. Nor does the nutritional thesis adequately account for the pattern of late nineteenth- and early twentieth-century mortality decline. If diet was so important why at a time of general advance in dietary standards did death rates from some infectious diseases fall while for others – croup, diphtheria, measles and infant diarrhoea, for example – they rose? In reality, variations in the incidence of major diseases such as cholera, smallpox and typhus appear to have owed little to variations in nutritional status. Even in the case of tuberculosis, where cohort, class and regional differentials in mortality are clearly to some extent influenced by varying standards of diet, death rates began to decline long before the onset of widespread improvements in nutrition.[33]

Claims for the primacy of the nutritional factor are no easier to confirm for the period after the First World War. Although improved standards of maternal nutrition obviously contributed to the continued decline in rates of maternal mortality after 1945, their contribution to the initial downturn in maternal death rates in the late 1930s and to regional variations in levels of maternal mortality ever since is thought to be minor compared with that of medical innovation and of changes in certain other conditions associated with poverty.[34] Work on the causes of international differentials in life expectancy during the 1900s, 1930s and 1960s likewise suggests that the main causes of mortality variation lie in factors other than changing levels of income and food per head.[35] In so far as standards of nutrition are determined by levels of real income, unemployment and poverty, the relationship between these variables and death rates has never been close enough to confirm the predominance of nutrition among the factors responsible for shaping mortality trends. To judge from data on the strength of the correlation between rates of infant mortality on the one hand and the income and occupation of fathers on the other, rising levels of per capita real income and declining levels of poverty made at least some contribution to the reduction in infant death rates that occurred in England and Wales in the decade immediately prior to the outbreak of the First World War. But, as indicated by the persistence of above average levels of infant mortality among miners, a relatively high income group, and below average levels of mortality among the infants of agricultural labourers, a relatively low income group, other factors were probably more influential.[36] While Brenner's analysis of mortality in England and Wales between 1936 and 1976 suggests a significant correlation between mortality rates and levels of unemployment, analyses based on arguably sounder statistical techniques by Stern and McAvinchey show the strength of the correlation to be much weaker.[37]

In fact, rising incomes and the new patterns of diet and consumption to which these gave rise may even have worked to increase deaths from certain causes. Coupled with the effects of technological innovation, greater consumer purchasing power permitted an ever-growing proportion of the population to eat, drink and smoke to excess, to avoid physical exercise and, until very recently, to switch their preferences from natural, high-fibre foods to less healthy diets based on convenience foods with a high fat content and excessive amounts of salt, sugar and artificial additives. It is no accident that in areas like Scotland and northern England and among lower status socio-occupational groups, where the incidence of alcoholism, cigarette smoking and fat consumption is greatest, death rates from 'diseases of affluence' such as lung cancer and heart disease are relatively high. The rise of such diseases to prominence in the disease aetiology of the later twentieth century may have been mainly no more than a secondary consequence of the decline in mortality from infectious disease, itself partly a result of improvements in nutrition. Yet there can also be no doubt that deaths from cancers and heart disease would have been lower had it not been for the new consumption habits made possible by the emergence of a more affluent society. An increase in the incidence of cigarette smoking between the First World War and the early 1960s was accompanied by a steady rise in mortality from lung cancer; rising levels of alcohol intake from the 1950s by an increase in deaths from alcohol-related diseases between the mid 1960s and mid 1980s; and higher levels of meat and fat consumption up to the early 1970s by an increase in mortality from heart disease. With the decline in cigarette and alcohol consumption, from the early 1960s and mid 1980s respectively, and the gradual replacement from the early 1970s of saturated by polyunsaturated fats, full cream milk by semi-skimmed milk and red meat by vegetarian foods in the popular diet, death rates from lung cancer and heart disease have decreased.[38] But for much of the twentieth century a combination of relatively high levels of cigarette smoking and a diet unusually rich in fat ensured that mortality from the two diseases in Britain was among the highest in the developed world.

If the part played by nutrition is less crucial than some have supposed, does a more satisfactory explanation of the mortality decline lie in the advances that have been made in the supply of medical institutions and personnel and the range and effectiveness of medical therapy and surgical technique?

For that part of the decline which occurred during the second half of the twentieth century, subsequent to the discovery and application of chemotherapeutical drugs from the later 1930s, the answer must be yes. The initial, sharp decline in rates of maternal mortality in 1936–7, for example, stemmed chiefly from the use of protonsil, the first of the sulphonamide drugs, in the treatment of puerperal fever: and it was largely as a result of further advances in medicine – the use of penicillin to treat septic abortion, the growing practice of blood transfusion, higher standards of midwifery following the Midwives Act of 1936, a greater emphasis on gynaecology in the training of medical students and general improvements in the quantity and quality of maternity services – that rates of maternal mortality continued to fall after the Second World War.[39] Most of the decline in perinatal death rates in England and Wales between 1950 and 1973 and in Scotland during the 1970s was due to improvements in obstetric practice and clinical management.[40] Beginning in the 1940s or 1950s deaths from respiratory diseases, whooping cough, enteric fever and tuberculosis were greatly reduced by the use of sulphyridine, sulphonamides, chloramphemicol, streptomycin and BCG immunisation. Around one-third of the decline in mortality from cardiovascular disease in recent decades was the result of drugs which reduced levels of blood pressure and cholesterol, beta blockers and anticoagulants and coronary bypass surgery, while improvements in diagnosis, drugs, surgery and radiation therapy have significantly reduced deaths from certain types of cancer. Even today, of course, there remain many causes of premature death that medicine cannot effectively overcome. But this should not be allowed to obscure the fact that innovations in medical therapy and surgical technique, facilitated by the creation of a National Health Service, made an important contribution to the continuing decline in death rates during the second half of the twentieth century.[41]

For the more substantial part of the modern mortality decline which had already occurred by the middle years of the century the contribution of medicine is more debatable.

If the role of medicine is interpreted solely in relation to the effectiveness of specific medical therapies and surgical techniques its significance was limited. Improvements in medicine and surgery were important to mortality decline only in the cases of appendicitis, peritonitis, smallpox, syphilis and deaths from causes other than micro-organisms, none of which figured prominently among the main causes of death in the late nineteenth and early twentieth centuries. For those infectious diseases whose decline contributed significantly to the rise in life expectation before the Second World War, effective, specific medical and surgical treatments were not available until the mid 1930s at the earliest.[42] A comparison of death rates in six different socio-economic sub-groups of the population of England and Wales between 1851 and 1911 confirms the view that medical advance made only a minor contribution to the initial phase of mortality decline.[43] To suggest, as some have, that declining rates of infant mortality in the period immediately before and during the First World War owed much to improved facilities for antenatal and post-natal maternal and child care and rising standards of mid-wifery following the Midwives Act of 1902 is to understate the difficulties involved in translating intention into reality. Despite the obvious growth in concern for mother and child welfare, standards of obstetric practice and antenatal and post-natal care improved very little before 1914 while the decline in infant death rates between 1914 and 1918, it has been suggested, far exceeded anything that might have been expected from the extent and quality of wartime infant and maternity welfare services. As late as the 1930s levels of obstetric knowledge and technique were so poor that they were more likely to increase than decrease death rates in childbirth. Even allowing for the contribution of innovations to which insufficient attention is usually paid – the growing use of anaesthetic, antiseptic and aseptic procedures in surgery, the discovery and application of a diphtheria antitoxin and an antimalaria serum, immunisation against tetanus and the use of insulin in the treatment of hormone deficiency diseases – it is difficult to dissent from the view that declining rates of infectious disease mortality in the first half of the twentieth century owed relatively little to advances in specific medical and surgical practice.[44]

It has recently been pointed out, however, that by concentrating solely on the role of specific medical and surgical techniques we run the risk of understating the contribution made by the medical profession. If the role of medicine is extended to include the pressure exerted by its members in favour of improvements in standards of personal hygiene and public health the significance of medicine is considerably enhanced. Through their involvement in the campaign for better housing, purer supplies of food and drink, improved methods of sewage disposal, higher standards of cleanliness and the more widespread adoption of efficient quarantine procedures, medical researchers and practitioners were crucial to the discovery and implementation of a range of environmental improvements which together were probably the single most important set of causes of increasing human longevity between the late nineteenth and mid twentieth centuries.[45]

To judge from the existence of a close, positive correlation between the extent of urbanisation on the one hand and levels of mortality on the other and also from the fact that, once begun, the pace of mortality decline was greater in urban than rural areas,[46] the principal explanation for the rise in life expectancy during the first half of the twentieth century lay in the success of initiatives designed to reduce excessive urban population densities and resolve the worst problems of food adulteration, housing, sanitation and disease control which inevitably accompanied them.

Some scholars, it is true, insist that the extent of environmental improvement was too limited to have had a significant impact on death rates. Winter, for instance, concludes that, though improved sanitation played a major role in the decline in mortality from waterborne infections, and legislation to combat food and drink adulteration a major role in the decline in infant mortality, overall, improvements in public health conditions and in the quality of food and drink products were, like innovations in medicine, secondary to rising standards of nutrition among the causes of increased longevity before the Second World War.[47] McKeown, Record and Turner reach a similar conclusion. Improvements in the quality of infant foods, water and milk and rising standards of sanitation, they claim, together accounted for no more than a sixth of the total reduction in death rates during the first half of the twentieth century. Most of the reduction was due to the effect of advances in nutrition and, to a lesser degree, medical therapy on the prevalence of airborne infections and causes of death other than those carried by food or water.[48]

Arguably, these interpretations are too pessimistic. Few would deny that the pace of environmental improvement was slow, particularly before the First World War, and that much remained to be done even in the 1950s. As late as 1914, despite a considerable body of permissive and sometimes compulsory legislation, little in practice had been achieved to resolve many of the worst problems of air and river pollution, urban overcrowding and working-class housing. Nevertheless, some effective steps had already been taken towards improving the nature of the environment in which people lived. The quality of food, milk and water supplies had risen. Methods of waste disposal had been improved by the drainage of cesspools and the introduction of dry conservancy and waterborne sewage systems and modern infiltration and treatment plants. The adoption of early notification procedures and the establishment of larger numbers of isolation hospitals had begun to combat the spread of contagious disease, and improvements in working conditions to reduce the incidence of industrial accidents and disease.

After 1914–18 the pace and range of environmental improvement increased. Of all the principal determinants of environmental quality only the quality of the urban air supply failed to improve in the course of the interwar period. Coupled with the trend towards smaller family sizes which began in the later nineteenth century and which, by lessening the risks of disease transmission, helped to reduce deaths from infectious diseases like measles, advances in public health conditions between the late nineteenth and mid twentieth centuries contributed more to the rise in human life expectancy than it has sometimes been usual to suppose. Cholera and typhoid succumbed primarily to the development of a purer water supply made possible by improvements in sewage systems. Deaths from non-respiratory tuberculosis and childhood diseases like scarlet fever declined under the impact of more regular and efficient quarantining practices. Drier and better ventilated housing, aided by the effect of falling fertility on infectious disease transmission rates, made a significant contribution to the decrease in mortality from respiratory tuberculosis and other airborne infections. A combination of purer drinking water, improvements in housing and methods of refuse disposal, the pasteurisation of milk and the increasing use of dried, powdered and unsweetened condensed milk as infant foods and the replacement of animal by motor transport, which reduced the scale of the urban dung problem, played an important part in the decline in deaths in infancy and childhood from diarrhoeal and related gastro-enteric infections.[49] In tandem with the benefits for health which accrued from the decline in family size, environmental improvements of this kind were influential elements in the continuous advance in human longevity through the first half of the twentieth century.[50]

Currently, perhaps the only acceptable explanation for the dramatic decline in mortality in the last hundred years or so is that it was the result of a complex variety of factors. Among those given the greatest emphasis in the literature are autonomous reductions in the virulence of disease viruses themselves, innovations in medicine, rising standards of public health, personal hygiene and housing and improved levels of nutrition. Less often stressed, but no less crucial, were the many factors which made all but the first of these possible: improvements in the education of mothers; more enlightened, less fatalistic attitudes towards ill-health and death; the emergence of central and local governments with the necessary authority and capability to pass and enforce medical and public health legislation; acceptance of the germ theory of disease; declining family size; the substitution of manual by non-manual, middle-class lifestyles with their greater stress on healthier eating, recreational exercise and lower fertility; and, above all, the technology and higher per capita incomes which came with economic modernisation and made so many of the proximate causes of a longer life feasible.[51] Beyond agreeing that autonomous factors were less important than those which originated in the actions of man and that the relative significance of each of the latter varied considerably by time, region and socio-occupational group there is, however, no consensus on the precise mix of causation. This is not surprising. So closely intertwined is the relationship between the various determinants of mortality that both in theory and practice it is difficult, perhaps impossible, to be more specific.

4

FERTILITY

Although lacking the precision of more sophisticated methods of measurement, the crude birth rate data (births per thousand total population) set out in Table 4.1 give an adequate indication of the main trends in overall levels of fertility in recent times.

As late as the third quarter of the nineteenth century crude birth rates were higher than in any other period of comparable length since at least the middle of the sixteenth century.[1] In the course of the decade beginning around 1876 they started to decline and, except for a brief interruption in the years immediately after the First World War, continued to decline until the late 1930s. In little more than 50 years birth rates in mainland Britain more than halved. Average numbers of births fell from between five and six for women born around 1870 to just two for women born around 1920. Except in eastern and southern Europe, where the onset of the fertility decline began later and where birth rates were still falling in the late 1930s, a similar trend occurred in many European countries.[2] Before 1911 the rate of decline was greater in some parts of Britain than others and the extent of pre-decline regional variation in birth rates temporarily widened. After 1911 regional birth rate differentials narrowed.[3] The result was that over the period from the mid 1870s to the late 1930s as a whole the decline in birth rates from one region to another was remarkably uniform and patterns of regional variation at the end of the interwar period remained much the same as those at the beginning of the century.[4]

In the years immediately prior to the outbreak of the Second World War crude birth rates began to rise, though the rise was less pronounced in Britain than in a number of other European countries. Total period fertility rates (defined as the number of children a woman would have had if she experienced current age-specific fertility rates throughout her reproductive span) reached their lowest level, 1.72, in 1933. By 1939 they had increased to 1.83.[5] Despite the fact that the exclusion of the British army from Europe for much of the war period helped keep fertility higher than it would otherwise have been, birth rates fell during the early years of the war but from 1941, in Scotland, and 1942, in England and Wales, once more began to rise. In the case of Scotland crude birth rates in the final year of the war were lower than they had ever been before. In the case of England and Wales however, though lower than in 1943 and 1944, they reached levels higher than at any time between 1931 and 1942. The repatriation of servicemen at the end of the war was accompanied by a sharp rise in fertility in 1946 and 1947. But from then until the mid 1950s birth rates declined. Between 1950 and 1955 total period fertility rates in England and Wales were among the lowest in Europe.[6]

Sometime around the mid 1950s fertility decline gave way to a surprising if moderate and shortlived increase. In England and Wales, where levels of total period fertility rose from a low of 2.14 in 1951 to a high of 2.94 in 1964, crude birth rates increased in each successive year between 1956 and 1964. Women born around 1937 and married by the early 1960s were the most fertile cohort of women born since the 1920s.[7] A similar, albeit less regular, increase in birth rates occurred in Scotland. The baby boom of the late 1950s and early 1960s was common to almost all countries in the developed world, but nowhere was it as pronounced as in Britain. The result was that by the mid 1960s rates of fertility in England and Wales were no longer among the lowest in Europe.[8]

In the second half of the 1960s baby boom was replaced by baby bust. From a peak of 18.5 per thousand in 1964 crude birth rates in England and Wales fell to a trough of 11.5 per thousand in 1977. Only among females in the youngest adult age groups did fertility continue to increase through the latter half of the 1960s, and even this tendency ceased from the early 1970s.[9] From 1978 the fertility of all socio-occupational groups in the population of England and Wales once again began to rise, though as late as 1990 birth rates were still only slightly higher than a decade or so earlier.[10] In Scotland crude birth rates fell from 20 per thousand in 1964 to 12 per thousand in 1977. Here, however, the extent of recovery in the late 1970s and 1980s was even less marked and persistent.[11]

Nearly everywhere in the developed world the evolution of fertility since the mid 1960s followed much the same pattern as in Britain. In most other European countries too the baby boom ended around 1964 or 1965 and rates of fertility decreased until the mid or late 1970s. Subsequently, while in most cases the decline in fertility either slowed or, as in Britain, gave way to modest fertility increase, there was rather more diversity of experience.[12] Everywhere, however, the preference for a two-child family structure remained intact.

Throughout the second half of the twentieth century, although the direction of birth rate trends was similar in almost all regions of mainland Britain, there remained some regional differences both in levels of aggregate fertility and in the rate at which these levels changed. From the 1960s to 1990 total period fertility rates were invariably higher in Scotland and the northern and midland regions of England than in the southern half of the country, and higher in regions with conurbations than elsewhere. In general, however, the extent of variation was small and, as in other European countries, tended to decline over time.[13] The tendency for regional fertility differentials to converge in the second half of the century is particularly evident in the change which took place in the relative levels of crude birth rates in England/Wales and Scotland. Between the beginning of the century and the early 1980s Scottish birth rates

Table 4.1 Annual average crude birth rates. England/Wales and Scotland, 1855–1990

	England/Wales	Scotland
1855	33.8	31.3
1860	34.3	35.6
1865	35.4	35.5
1870	35.2	34.6
1875	35.4	35.2
1880	34.2	33.6
1885	32.9	32.7
1890	30.2	30.4
1895	30.3	30.0
1900	28.7	29.6
1905	27.3	28.6
1910	25.1	26.2
1915	21.9	23.9
1920	25.5	28.1
1925	18.3	21.4
1930	16.3	19.6
1935	14.7	17.8
1940	14.1	17.1
1945	15.9	16.9
1950	15.8	18.1
1955	15.0	18.1
1960	17.1	19.6
1965	18.1	19.3
1970	16.0	16.8
1975	12.2	13.1
1980	13.2	13.4
1985	13.1	13.0
1990	13.9	12.9

Sources: B. R. Mitchell, *British Historical Statistics* (Cambridge, 1988), pp. 42–7. CSO, *Annual Abstract of Statistics 1993* (London, 1993), pp. 27–8.

consistently exceeded those in England and Wales. From the late 1960s, however, the differential began to narrow and by the late 1970s was barely perceptible. By 1983–90, as had been the case through much of the second half of the nineteenth century, crude birth rates and rates of total period fertility in Scotland had fallen below those in England and Wales.[14]

Illegitimacy

Variations in levels of overall fertility are a product of variations in one or other of three demographic mechanisms – the number of births outside marriage (illegitimacy), ages at marriage and the proportions married (nuptiality), and the frequency of childbirth within marriage (marital fertility).

From at least as early as the middle of the sixteenth century levels of illegitimacy have varied considerably by social class, region and time. In the twentieth century, as in previous centuries, illegitimacy has been predominantly a working-class phenomenon. In 1983, for example, over three-quarters of all illegitimates were born to women in the manual occupational groups of the population, more than a third of the total to women in social class V.[15] Levels of bastardy in England throughout the period between the late sixteenth and late twentieth centuries were consistently higher in western and northern than southern and south-eastern counties.[16] Thus, in 1981, English illegitimacy ratios (illegitimates per hundred live births) ranged from 9.5 in East Anglia to 10.3 in the South West, 12.6 in the South East and East Midlands, 12.8 in the West Midlands, 13.2 in the North, 13.5 in Yorkshire/Humberside and 15.5 in the North West. In 1990 the range of variation ran from a low of 22.8 in East Anglia to 24.3 in the South West, 25.9 in the South East, 28.0 in the East Midlands, 30.6 in Yorkshire/Humberside, 32.5 in the West Midlands, 32.8 in the North and 34.5 in the North West.[17] In Scotland between the mid nineteenth and mid twentieth centuries illegitimacy ratios were always relatively high in midland, south-eastern and south-western counties, lowest in northern and north-western counties and, unusually, higher among rural than urban populations. Only after the mid 1950s did levels of bastardy in Scottish urban areas rise above those in rural areas.[18]

Trends in levels of illegitimacy since the middle of the nineteenth century are summarised in Table 4.2. Down to the
middle of the twentieth century illegitimacy ratios in Scotland
exceeded those in England and Wales. The differential narrowed in the years immediately following the Second World
War and from the 1950s onwards was largely reversed. In every
year from 1952 to 1990, with the exception of 1973, 1975 and
1976, bastardy ratios in Scotland were lower than in England
and Wales.

Despite this, both countries experienced a very similar
trend. In England levels of illegitimacy were already beginning
to fall in the 1840s. In Scotland the decline began in the
1860s. By 1900 the proportion of live births born outside marriage was a third lower than half a century earlier. From then
until the 1950s illegitimacy ratios fluctuated around a relatively unchanging trend. Sometime around 1960 they began
to rise. The rise was particularly rapid between the late 1950s
and late 1960s and in the 1980s. Between the late 1960s and
late 1970s, perhaps because the easier availability of legal abortion made possible by the 1967 Abortion Act allowed the ter-
mination of some of the pregnancies that might otherwise
have resulted in an illegitimate birth, it was more muted. The
increase in illegitimacy during the 1980s, an increase shared
by all regions and social classes, was quite extraordinary and
greater in Britain than in all other European countries except
France and the Republic of Ireland. By 1990 in excess of one
in four children were born outside wedlock, a ratio more than
twice that of a decade earlier.[19]

Broadly similar trends in illegitimacy occurred in most
developed countries of the world. Between 1880 and 1940
levels of bastardy declined nearly everywhere in Europe.[20]
From around 1960 they rose. In some countries, mainly
located in eastern and southern Europe, the rise was negligible or, at most, small. In others, chiefly in northern and
western Europe, it was more marked – in the cases of Belgium,
Denmark, East Germany, France, the Irish Republic, the
Netherlands, Norway and Sweden even greater than in
Britain.[21] Actual levels of illegitimacy, of course, have

Table 4.2 Illegitimacy ratios (illegitimate births per hundred live births). England/Wales and Scotland, 1855–1990

	England/Wales	Scotland
1855	6.5	7.8
1860	6.4	9.2
1865	6.3	10.0
1870	5.7	9.5
1875	4.8	8.7
1880	4.9	8.5
1885	4.8	8.5
1890	4.4	7.6
1895	4.2	7.3
1900	4.0	6.5
1905	4.0	6.9
1910	4.1	7.3
1915	4.5	6.9
1920	1.6	7.5
1925	4.1	6.5
1930	4.6	7.3
1935	4.2	6.5
1940	4.4	5.9
1945	9.3	7.7
1950	5.0	5.2
1955	4.6	4.3
1960	5.5	4.3
1965	7.8	5.6
1970	8.2	7.7
1975	9.0	9.3
1980	11.7	11.2
1985	19.2	18.5
1990	28.3	27.1

Sources: B. R. Mitchell, *British Historical Statistics* (Cambridge, 1988), pp. 42–7. Registrar-General Scotland, *Annual Report 1991* (Edinburgh, 1992), p. 19. OPCS, 'Tables', *Population Trends*, 68 (1992), 47.
J. Cooper, 'Births Outside Marriage: Recent Trends and Associated Demographic and Social Changes', *Population Trends*, 63 (1991), 9.

continued to vary substantially from one country to another. Throughout the first half of the twentieth century illegitimacy ratios in the United Kingdom were comparatively low and as late as 1956–60 still lower than in 12 of 21 European countries.

By 1966–70 they were exceeded in only 7 of 23 European states and by 1990 only in the northern European countries of Denmark, Iceland and Finland.[22]

The causes of variations in bastardy remain obscure. The fact that trends in illegitimacy followed much the same pattern from one country to another has led some historians to presume the existence of a common explanation. But even if this presumption is justified there is as yet no agreement on what this common explanation, or common set of explanations, was. For the time being, therefore, the only sensible course to pursue in the search for causation is to proceed country by country. Why then did levels of illegitimacy in Britain decline between the mid nineteenth and mid twentieth centuries and rise in the second half of the twentieth century, with particular rapidity in the 1980s?

Some possible explanations can be speedily dismissed. Among these must be included variations in the extent of urbanisation and industrialisation, in the numerical balance between the sexes and in levels of material prosperity, nutrition and health and the effects these had on rates of fecundity, ages at menarche and the incidence of spontaneous abortion or stillbirth.[23] Nor, it seems, should too much significance be attached to the part played by variations in the extent of courtship activity and in the size of what has been called 'the sub-society of the bastard-prone'. Periods of relative economic prosperity, it is argued, were accompanied not only by higher rates of nuptiality and marital fertility but also by an increase in the extent of sexual intercourse among the unmarried and a substantially greater rate of growth in the fertility of women who bore children outside wedlock than in that of women who bore children within marriage.[24] Intriguing though this thesis is, it has to be said that for the twentieth century anyway it lacks consistent empirical support. While low and relatively constant illegitimacy ratios between the late nineteenth century and the 1930s conformed with a period of low and relatively constant rates of nuptiality and rising illegitimacy ratios between the late 1950s and late 1960s with a period of rising nuptiality, no such relationship between the two variables was apparent in the 1970s, and in the 1980s, when illegitimacy ratios increased dramatically, levels of nuptiality actually fell.

Other potential explanations are less easily dismissed. In their explanation for the emergence and persistence of low rates of bastardy between the late nineteenth and mid twentieth centuries, for instance, Tilly, Scott and Cohen stress the contributions made by declining numbers of sexually vulnerable female domestic servants, reductions in the flow of female migrants to towns and cities and, above all, the growth of working-class prosperity which worked to restrict illegitimacy by reducing the number of young women away from their families, facilitating marriage and reducing the population of highly mobile, propertyless men whose need constantly to move in search of employment had increased the likelihood that pregnancy would not be followed by marriage.[25] Admittedly, in this case too, the argument is offered as an hypothesis with little or no empirical confirmation and one aspect of it – the suggestion that illegitimacy ratios correlated positively with numbers of female domestic servants – receives no support from Crafts' analysis of interurban differentials in bastardy in England and Wales in 1911 where the presence of a large population of female domestic servants was accompanied by low, not high, levels of illegitimacy. On the other hand the fact that low levels of income and employment among women in 1911 correlated with high rates of illegitimacy, coupled with the fact that regional variations in illegitimacy in England and Wales 70 years later were positively related to variations in levels of male unemployment and the proportion of the labour force in unskilled occupations, suggests that what Tilly, Scott and Cohen have to say about the implications for bastardy of increased working-class prosperity should not be dismissed too readily.[26]

Long-term variations in levels of illegitimacy may also have owed something to a combination of changes in the nature of birth control technology and changes in attitudes towards premarital sex and the institution of marriage. According to this interpretation the two phases of abnormally high and rising rates of illegitimacy in modern times, the first in the late eighteenth and early nineteenth centuries and the second between the 1960s and 1980s, were chiefly the result of a dramatic increase in the extent of sexual promiscuity among the unmarried. During the first phase greater opportunities for employment, and thus for financial independence, liberated young, single women from the customary control of parents and community and allowed them to indulge in a degree of sexual licence never before possible. In the absence of effective, or effectively practised, birth control technologies the consequence was a sharp rise in the number of children born outside wedlock. When, between the late nineteenth and mid twentieth centuries, methods of birth control improved and the practice of birth control became more acceptable, levels of illegitimacy declined. A further increase in the extent of premarital sexual activity, this time prompted by the revolt of a new youth culture against parental authority and traditional norms of social behaviour, occurred in the 1960s. Because contraception was practised less efficiently by the unmarried than the married, this too was accompanied by another surge in rates of bastardy.[27]

The belief that secular trends in illegitimacy were essentially a function of changes in the incidence of extramarital sexual intercourse has been hotly disputed, principally on the grounds that the only evidence offered in support of variations in levels of sexual activity outside marriage is the variations which occurred in levels of illegitimacy themselves.[28] At least for the twentieth century, however, there is some reason to suppose that the rejection of what has come to be known as the Shorter thesis is premature and probably unjustified. Lower rates of premarital conception in the 1950s than in Victorian times, together with the continued rarity of extramarital cohabitation and divorce, imply that until well into the second half of the twentieth century commitment to the values of married life, a commitment reinforced by the psychological impact of the two world wars,[29] was too strong to permit widespread sexual intercourse outside marriage. The sudden surge in premarital conception rates in the late 1950s and early 1960s and rising levels of extramarital cohabitation and divorce from the 1960s and 1970s, by contrast, imply the recent emergence of more liberal attitudes towards nonmarital sexual intercourse.[30] Some confirmation of this is provided by the results of survey data on the extent of sexual intercourse among unmarried women. As late as the 1950s and early 1960s fewer than one in three women admitted to having had sex before marriage. By the end of the 1960s the figure had risen to 60 per cent and ten years later to between 80 and 90 per cent. In the space of little more than a decade sexual intercourse outside marriage had become the typical rather than the atypical experience.[31] As late as the early 1970s the usual outcome of a premarital conception was marriage. By the 1980s abortion or illegitmacy were the more likely consequences.[32] In part this stemmed from the emergence of a value system which attached more importance to the wishes and interests of the individual than to those of the family or the community and which therefore allowed greater individual freedom of choice in behaviour.[33] But, in part, it was also a secondary consequence of the decline in rates of nuptiality which occurred during the 1970s and 1980s, and the forces responsible for it. As the proportion of women living outside marriage increased, so too did levels of extramarital sexual intercourse and illegitimacy.[34]

Nuptiality

Before the last quarter of the nineteenth century temporal, regional and socio-occupational class differences in rates of fertility were mainly determined by differences in levels of nuptiality. Since the mid 1870s, though nuptiality has continued to have an influence, the behaviour of aggregate fertility has been determined chiefly by what happened to marital fertility.[35]

Between the middle of the nineteenth century and the early 1930s crude marriage rates (marriages per thousand total population), average ages at marriage and the proportions never married fluctuated around levels that had been typical of British and western European nuptiality experience since at least the seventeenth century. It follows that the nuptiality mechanism could have played no more than a minor role in the novel, long-term decline in rates of overall fertility which began in the mid 1870s.[36]

In stark contrast the period between the 1930s and the start of the 1970s saw the creation of 'a new marriage pattern... which had not been seen in the west for centuries'.[37] In all social groups ages at marriage and the percentages of men and women remaining unmarried in each age group declined and crude marriage rates rose. Similar increases in nuptiality occurred in many other industrialised countries of the European and non-European world.[38] Because of improvements in the ratio of men to women caused by changes in the balance and sex structure of international migration and the absence of male mortality rates on the scale of the First World War, the increase in nuptiality in the several decades leading up to the early 1970s was especially marked among females.[39] All scholars agree that this tendency towards earlier and more universal marriage contributed significantly to the baby boom of the late 1950s and early 1960s and perhaps accounted for as much as 30 per cent of the rise in aggregate fertility rates between 1930 and the mid 1960s.[40]

Since the early 1980s, in line with what happened in most industrialised countries, crude marriage rates have fallen, average ages at marriage have risen and, at least in the age groups 16–29, the proportions marrying have declined. Despite this, at the end of the 1980s Britain still boasted one of the youngest marital age patterns in western Europe and marriage remained the ultimate preference for the great majority of people.[41]

As Table 4.3 shows, from at least as early as the middle of the nineteenth century down to the outbreak of the Second World War, crude marriage rates were consistently higher in England and Wales than in Scotland. In two out of every three years between 1941 and 1990, by contrast, marriage rates were higher, and marriage earlier, in Scotland. A similar trend towards less regional diversity in nuptiality experience

Table 4.3 Annual average crude marriage rates. England/Wales and Scotland, 1855–1990

	England/Wales	Scotland
1855	16.2	13.2
1860	17.1	13.9
1865	17.5	14.8
1870	16.1	14.3
1875	16.7	14.8
1880	14.9	13.2
1885	14.5	13.1
1890	15.5	13.7
1895	15.0	13.5
1900	16.0	14.6
1905	15.3	13.6
1910	15.0	13.0
1915	19.4	15.2
1920	20.2	19.2
1925	15.2	13.3
1930	15.8	13.8
1935	17.2	15.3
1940	22.5	21.2
1945	18.7	18.9
1950	16.3	15.8
1955	16.1	16.9
1960	15.0	15.5
1965	15.5	15.6
1970	17.0	16.6
1975	15.4	15.1
1980	14.9	14.9
1985	13.9	14.2
1990	13.1	13.6

Sources: B. R. Mitchell, *British Historical Statistics* (Cambridge, 1988), pp. 72–4. CSO, *Annual Abstract of Statistics 1993* (London, 1993), pp. 22–3.

emerged in most European countries in the course of the twentieth century.[42]

Accompanying these changes in the incidence of and age at marriage were equally notable changes in the extent of divorce, remarriage and extramarital cohabitation.

Until the late 1950s rates of divorce remained negligible. Thereafter they began to rise, slowly at first and then, from the late 1960s, more rapidly. In England and Wales the number of divorces per thousand married couples increased from around two in 1961 to six in 1971, around twelve in 1981 and, following a period of relative stability in the early 1980s, around thirteen between 1985 and 1990. In Scotland, where divorce rates were always slightly lower, they likewise rose to a peak in 1985 (11.2) before settling at between 9.8 and 10.7 in the second half of the 1980s. These trends were repeated everywhere in the industrialised world.[43] Generally, levels of divorce have varied inversely with social class and, except for those in personal service, artistic, literary, sporting, security and selling occupations, have invariably been higher among manual than non-manual workers.[44]

Throughout the first half of the twentieth century, when rates of adult mortality were lower than they had ever been before, and divorce a rarity, the incidence of remarriage was low. Since the late 1970s, as a result of rising divorce rates, its incidence has greatly increased. Between 1965 and 1988 the proportion of marriages in England and Wales involving at least one previously married partner rose from 16 to 37 per cent.[45] As a proportion of all divorced men and women, however, rates of remarriage fell by a third in the 1970s and continued to fall in the 1980s.[46] The reason for this was that divorced people increasingly preferred cohabitation outside marriage. Until the early 1970s only about one in twenty married couples had lived together before marriage. Ten years later the figure had soared to over a quarter and by the end of the 1980s to half of all first-married couples and nearly three-quarters of all remarried couples. Simultaneously, the average length of time spent cohabiting increased from nine months in the 1970s to fifteen months in the 1980s.[47]

The persistence of relatively low levels of nuptiality in the period before the 1930s was the consequence of a complex mix of demographic and economic circumstances. One of the most important of these was the excess of women over men in the marriageable age groups, itself a product of higher rates of male than female mortality and of the disproportionate share of males in net overseas emigration flows in the decades immediately before and after the First World War. Housing shortages, high levels of male unemployment, restricted opportunities for the employment of married women and, to extend an argument advanced by Friedlander to explain the decline in nuptiality between 1873 and 1896, a general mood of economic insecurity provided additional reasons for postponing or even abandoning marriage.[48]

Economic circumstances also go some way towards explaining why in the course of the first half of the twentieth century regional differentials in nuptiality experiences narrowed. At the beginning of the century, when many local economies were still weakly integrated into national economic systems, spatial variation in nuptiality and other demographic characteristics was inevitable. In Scotland between 1861 and 1914, for instance, levels of nuptiality were always highest in regions where the pace of economic growth was greatest and opportunities for employment most abundant. Lower levels of nuptiality in Scotland than in England and Wales between the mid nineteenth and mid twentieth centuries likewise owed much to differences in economic conditions, in this case especially to the unusually high ratio of live-in farmworkers in the Scottish labour force and the relatively limited opportunities afforded by the Scottish economy for employment in mining and heavy industry.[49] Even in the late twentieth century regional variations in percentages married in England and Wales were partly determined by variations in male wage levels.[50] Of course, as Watkins reminds us, economic factors were not the only ones at work. In addition to the influence exerted by the forces of market integration, labour migration and transport improvement, the decline in regional nuptiality differentials also owed a good deal to the development of mass communications systems, the promotion of a stronger sense of national unity during the depression of the 1930s and the two world wars and the creation by central governments of more uniform, nation-wide institutions for education and welfare.[51]

The determinants of nuptiality trends since the 1930s are no less complex and the relative importance of each no less difficult to assess. Some were of only limited or short-lived significance. In this category might be included advances in state social welfare provision which facilitated marriage by alleviating the worse effects of unemployment and low incomes; further growth in the acceptability of 'artificial' contraceptive practices and the greater availability and lower cost of contraceptive technology which made it easier to control family size without having to postpone or deny the pleasures of marriage; improvements in the numerical balance between the sexes brought about by changes in the relationship between levels of in- and out-migration; increases in the stock of public sector housing in the 1950s and 1960s; and the role of wartime propaganda and psychology in reinforcing the traditional emphasis on woman's domestic function and the virtues of family life and in encouraging a desire for higher rates of fertility in the economic and political interests of Britain and her Empire.[52] All these, it has been argued, contributed in some measure to the unmistakable rise in nuptiality rates which occurred between the 1930s and early 1970s.

To some historians, however, rising levels of nuptiality in the 1950s and 1960s owed most to the fact that these were decades of unprecedentedly high incomes and full employment, particularly for teenagers and young adults. At precisely the time rising standards of health were acting to reduce the age of sexual maturity and thus the age at which the desire for a regular sexual relationship within marriage began, rising real incomes were acting to make this desire easier to fulfil.[53] When, in subsequent decades, levels of unemployment increased and the pace of per capita real income growth slackened, high rates of nuptiality became more difficult to sustain, marriage rates fell and ages at marriage rose.

If only because of its simplicity and apparent fit with the empirical evidence, this interpretation of nuptiality trends in the second half of the twentieth century is appealing. Arguably, however, it oversimplifies the nature of the relationship between variations in employment and prosperity on the one hand and variations in nuptiality on the other. Indirectly, by promoting individualism and greater levels of tolerance for individual nonconformity and by raising the real costs involved in searching out a suitable partner, rearing children and providing the goods and services essential for a satisfying family life, rising levels of prosperity in the 1950s and 1960s may have worked to discourage rather than encourage marriage.[54] Mindful of this most historians are inclined to believe that a more acceptable explanation of nuptiality trends after the Second World War lies in what happened to the relationship between the earning power of men and women.

In the period between 1945 and the early 1970s, partly because demographic changes increased the ratio of female to male workers and partly because most of the growth in employment opportunities was concentrated in the service sectors of the economy where women were in particular demand, women's wages decreased drastically in relation to those of men. As the relative earnings of women declined, the amount of income lost by women in preferring marriage and children to paid employment diminished, and marriage became an increasingly attractive proposition, all the more so since, in terms of income foregone, time spent on domestic duties is less costly when supplied solely by the no- or low-wage spouse. In the course of the first half of the 1970s, by contrast, the ratio of female to male wages rose and, despite periodic fluctuations, has remained higher than in the 1950s and 1960s ever since. As the relative earnings of women increased, the attractions of marriage lessened, ages at marriage rose and marriage rates fell.[55]

The recent decline in levels of nuptiality, of course, has not been entirely due to changes in economic circumstances. Rising rates of divorce and a growing preference for cohabitation outside marriage, and the forces responsible for them, have also played a part. One of the factors responsible for the recent increase in divorce rates in Britain and elsewhere in the developed world was the widespread liberalisation of divorce laws in the 1960s and 1970s which facilitated the legal dissolution of unsatisfactory marriages. The fundamental cause, however, was those forces which made the introduction of more liberal divorce legislation possible. One of these was falling mortality, which increased the average duration of married life and thus the likelihood of marital disharmony. Another was the Second World War which, by subjecting marriages to long periods of separation and increasing the number of marriages entered into with undue haste, enhanced both the potential for marital breakdown and the desire for easier divorce legislation. Reductions in male and female earnings differentials since the early 1970s have added a further impetus to the growing frequency of divorce. As their relative incomes rose, married women became less willing to continue in unsatisfactory unions and better able to withdraw from them. But perhaps the most influential force at work was the changes which occurred during the 1960s and 1970s in the underlying philosophies of individual and family life. The belief that the institution of marriage was inviolable was only one of the many facets of traditional social and cultural organisation and custom to fall prey to a system of values that increasingly emphasised individual free choice at the expense of the dictates of family, church and state.

Once divorce rates began to increase they exerted their own depressive impact on levels of nuptiality. Divorce is emotionally as well as financially draining. As its incidence grew, the expected gains from marriage diminished and a preference for extramarital cohabitation increased. For ever-larger numbers of people cohabitation was seen as an ideal vehicle for acquiring the additional information needed to minimise the risks of divorce and improve the likelihood that marriage would bring the benefits anticipated. In tandem with the effects of increasing sexual activity outside marriage, the availability of more effective methods of contraception which lessened the chances of nonmarital pregnancy and, in the 1980s, a resurgence of housing shortages and the introduction of less generous laws relating to mortgage tax relief, this attitude was sufficient to promote informal cohabitation at the expense of formal marriage.[56]

Marital Fertility

Allowing for some contribution from variations in nuptiality,[57] temporal, regional and socio-occupational differentials in aggregate fertility between the late nineteenth and late twentieth centuries were determined primarily by variations in the extent and frequency of childbirth within marriage. Down to the mid 1870s levels of marital fertility in England and Wales fluctuated around a more or less unchanging trend. In the ten years following 1876, at roughly the same rate in every region of the country, they began to decline and continued to decline until the 1930s.[58] In Scotland rates of marital fertility between the mid nineteenth century and the 1930s were higher than in England and Wales, but here too began to fall from the mid 1870s and more rapidly from the mid 1880s. Despite a growing tendency for childbirth to be compressed into an ever shorter time-span early in married life, from the mid 1950s to the mid 1960s, partly because of an earlier start to childbearing among married couples and partly because of a decline in the percentage of childless and single-child marriages, rates of marital fertility rose. Sometime around the mid 1960s, as a result of an increase in the number of permanently childless marriages but principally because of a reduction in the number of families with three or more children, rates of marital fertility once more started to decline. By the 1980s intervals between births were so protracted and the onset of childbearing so long delayed that in all socio-occupational groups a substantial divergence had emerged between the reproductive behaviour of females in their teens and twenties, whose fertility rates fell, and that of females in their thirties and early forties, whose fertility rose. The divergence was especially noticeable among females in social classes I and II. Similar trends in marital fertility since the Second World War were evident throughout western Europe and much of the rest of the developed world.[59]

Even before 1914 regional variations in levels of marital fertility in England and Wales were modest and steadily decreasing. By the early 1930s low rates of fertility within marriage were the norm almost everywhere. In Scotland, though less marked than on the continent of Europe, regional marital fertility differentials were more pronounced than in England and Wales and widened between the 1870s and the outbreak of the Second World War. In some of the more remote parts of the Scottish Highlands, indeed, levels of marital fertility remained high until well into the 1930s. After 1945, however, in Scotland as elsewhere in Europe regional variations in marital fertility rates markedly decreased.[60]

Differences in rates of marital fertility by socio-occupational class long pre-dated the onset of the modern fertility decline in the mid 1870s. During the initial stages of the transition to lower fertility, from the mid 1870s to the First World War, the differences probably widened. Since the First World War, as elsewhere in western Europe, they have narrowed. Until the middle of the twentieth century the fertility of married couples varied inversely with social class, rising from its lowest level in social class I (mainly the highest status professional occupations) to progressively higher levels in social classes II (managers, senior administrators and other professional occupations of intermediate status), IIIN (non-manual workers such as clerks and salesmen), IIIM (skilled manual workers), IV (the semi-skilled) and V (the unskilled). By the second half of the century rates of marital fertility in social class II had fallen below those in social class I and were lowest of all in social class IIIN. Otherwise, in broad terms at least, fertility differentials within marriage have continued to correlate negatively with socio-occupational status.[61]

Causes of Marital Fertility Decline

Why did rates of marital fertility decline between the mid 1870s and the 1930s and why have they remained low ever since?

At its most superficial level the explanation lies in the increasing awareness, acceptability, availability and application of ever-more effective techniques for limiting the frequency of conception. Birth control practices within marriage were not, of course, wholly new to the late nineteenth and twentieth centuries. What was new was an unprecedented growth in the willingness of married couples to resort to them. Spurred on by the publicity given to the Bradlaugh–Besant trial of 1877 and, subsequently, by the spread of more liberal attitudes to sex provoked by the First World War and the work of Marie Stopes in the immediate postwar years, popular appreciation of the aims and means of family planning increased dramatically. For the first time the advocacy and adoption of 'artificial' methods of contraception within marriage became publicly acceptable. By the 1930s, if only when it could be justified on health grounds, even those bastions of sexual conservatism, the Anglican church and the British Medical Association, were prepared to advocate birth control practices.[62]

Accompanying these advances in awareness and acceptability were advances in the accessibility and efficiency of birth control technology itself. Most of the innovations in contraceptive techniques before the First World War – the rubber condom, the Dutch cap, the douche and chemical spermicides of one kind or another – were expensive or difficult to utilise and therefore restricted mainly to upper- and middle-class sections of society. On the whole, those working-class couples who had already begun to reduce their fertility continued to rely on abortion, abstention or the less reliable method of *coitus interruptus*, a fact which goes some way towards explaining why social class differentials in fertility widened during the initial phase of the modern fertility decline. By the interwar period the new mechanical and chemical methods of contraception were less costly and more accessible and, as a result, working-class fertility began to decline more rapidly. After the Second World War innovations such as the female contraceptive pill, the coil and sterilisation further improved the cost-effectiveness of birth control technology and helped continue the progress towards narrower differentials in socio-occupational class fertility rates.

All scholars are agreed that improvements in birth control methods played some part in making the transition to lower levels of marital fertility possible. At the same time, given that traditional rather than modern techniques of contraception remained the dominant means of family limitation throughout the period down to the middle of the twentieth century when the bulk of the fertility decline occurred,[63] it would be unwise to accord them too much importance. According to Crafts, advances in birth control technology and reductions in the real cost of modern contraceptive devices accounted for no more than half of the decline in levels of fertility which occurred in England and Wales between 1895 and 1938, a view shared by most other students of the phenomenon.[64]

In any case, whether it involved the more widespread application of old methods or the adoption of new ones, contraception was merely the *instrument* by which lower levels of marital fertility were brought about. The crucial questions are why birth control techniques were more extensively adopted and why lower fertility norms became desirable.

From the outset attempts to answer these questions have focused on various aspects of the process of modernisation. This is not to deny that there have been occasions when reductions in fertility were designed to preserve rather than to destroy traditional values and customs. Interpretations of the fertility decline couched simply in terms of the effects of a transition from traditional to modern productive, attitudinal and behavioural systems can sometimes be misleading. In the case of the Sicilian peasantry, for instance, the adoption of lower fertility norms was intended to protect age-old traditions which, for various reasons, were becoming increasingly difficult to sustain.[65] Even in these cases, however, the achievement of lower fertility would not have been possible without at least some of the prerequisites for fertility control which originated in the process of modernisation. Generally there can be no doubt that the fertility transition was a corollary of modernisation, broadly defined, and would have been inconceivable without it.[66] The problem has always been to identify those facets of the modernisation process that were most responsible. Was the fertility transition chiefly a response to prior reductions in levels of infant and child mortality? Was it mainly a consequence of the changes in economic and social structures which accompanied modernisation and, if so, of which ones in particular? Or was it principally due to changes in ideational systems which emerged independently of the process of modern economic development?

In theory there is every reason to suppose a close relationship between levels of fertility and levels of mortality in infancy and childhood. The lower the rate of mortality in infancy and childhood the greater the need for parents to limit their fertility in the interests of ensuring that the financial and emotional costs of children do not exceed what they can afford. Lower infant and child death rates also reduce the necessity for couples to bear large numbers of children in order to ensure support in old age and, at the same time, increase the amount of emotional energy they lavish on children. A child-centred family culture of the kind that had emerged by the early twentieth century, it has been argued, is only feasible when infant and child survival rates are high enough to make it worthwhile for parents to invest considerable time and affection on their offspring.

In practice the extent to which the fertility transition depended on a prior decline in infant and child mortality has provoked much dispute. Chesnais has recently concluded that, though by no means the only factor involved, the reduction in mortality in infancy and early childhood should be given principal responsibility for the trend to lower fertility norms. Indeed, had it not been for the part played by overseas emigration in relieving Britain and other European countries of an excess population caused by falling mortality, the fertility transition may have begun even earlier, and proceeded more rapidly, than it did.[67]

Few scholars have been prepared to go quite so far, though most accept that declining infant and child mortality did make a significant contribution to the adoption of lower fertility schedules.[68] For some, however, even this is to claim too much. It has been pointed out, for instance, that variations in marital fertility by socio-occupational class in England and Wales in the period 1870–1914 were only partially related to variations in infant and child death rates.[69] Cross-sectional analysis of data for the urban populations of England and Wales in 1911 indicates only a weak correlation between fertility and levels of mortality in infancy and childhood, suggesting that the contribution of declining mortality to the decrease in marital fertility between the mid 1870s and the late 1930s was minimal.[70] Within each region of England and Wales, moreover, temporal fluctuations in fertility and rates of mortality in early childhood were so closely synchronised that it is difficult to see how couples could have been basing their subsequent reproductive decisions on the mortality experience of previous births. Throughout the late nineteenth and first half of the twentieth centuries national and regional trends in infant and child death rates were always more variable than those in marital fertility and, whereas in the course of the period regional differentials in mortality diminished, those in fertility did not. In at least one sub-period, 1885–98, while fertility rates fell in every region of England and Wales, rates of child mortality rose in some regions, fell in others and for England and Wales as a whole altered little. None of this suggests that the contribution of declining infant and child death rates to the fertility transition deserves special emphasis.[71] If survival rates early in life were as crucial to fertility decisions as some believe, why did the trend to lower fertility not begin earlier in rural areas, where mortality in infancy and childhood was relatively low, than in urban areas, where it was relatively high? The answer must be that there are determinants of reproductive behaviour more important than levels of mortality in the first year or so of life.

Among the most influential of these was the process of economic modernisation. Declining rates of infant and child mortality, of course, were themselves largely a consequence of the rising standards of nutrition, medical care and personal and public hygiene made possible by advances in education, technology and wealth. Of more direct and critical significance for trends in marital fertility, however, were the effects of modern economic growth on levels of real income, the extent and character of female employment, patterns of income distribution, the availability of consumer goods and the structure of the family economy.

The implications for marital fertility of rising levels of per capita real income depend on the nature of the environment within which the latter occur.[72] When not accompanied by changes in tastes, costs and knowledge, higher real incomes make it easier to support additional children and act to promote fertility. Where they help to widen the range of consumer choice and are accompanied by a need for children of improved quality and therefore greater cost, they work to alter patterns of parental expenditure in ways that are inimical to fertility.[73] As one scholar has put it, while the direct effects of economic growth tend to encourage procreation, the indirect, or social, effects of economic growth tend to discourage it.[74] In economies and socio-occupational groups where incomes are close to subsistence and the range of goods and services available as alternatives to children are relatively restricted, a rise in per capita income is more likely to increase than decrease fertility, hence the apparent rise in birth rates during the initial stages of the British Industrial Revolution.[75] By the late nineteenth century the economic environment within which fertility decisions were taken was very different. For the bulk of the population continued economic growth, assisted by the import of cheap food from the countries of the New World, had lifted incomes comfortably above basic subsistence levels and broadened the range of goods and services available for purchase as alternatives to children. The result was that more people than ever before were in a position to choose between expenditures on children and expenditures on material goods or leisure activities. Increasingly they chose the latter. Before the First World War the contribution of rising incomes to the decline in fertility in England and Wales was probably modest and in Scotland rates of marital fertility remained highest in regions where the pace of economic growth and opportunities for employment were greatest. By the interwar period, however, it was usually regions and occupations with the lowest per capita incomes and highest rates of unemployment, where additional children were less likely to be seen as a threat to improvements in living standards, that had the highest fertility levels.[76] To the extent that economic growth and rising real incomes were accompanied by increased rates of social mobility and a decline in regional, and especially rural-urban, income differentials, the range of conditions favourable to reductions in marital fertility widened still further.[77]

One of the features of economic modernisation given particular emphasis in recent explanations of the modern fertility decline is the changes that have taken place in the extent and character of women's employment. The explanation stems from the observation that socio-occupational differentials in fertility relate inversely to the proportion of women in paid employment outside the home; in coalmining populations, where women were rarely gainfully employed, fertility was relatively high; in the textile industries, where women were more extensively employed, fertility was relatively low.[78] Most of the increase in female employment opportunities in the first half of the twentieth century was confined to unmarried women. As the employment of single women in manufacturing industry, technical and clerical services and the professions increased while that in home-based occupations like domestic service decreased, so they became more independent and more exposed to the liberating influences of higher wages, more leisure time and the greater knowledge generated by increased contact with the media and other females. Together these influences ensured that marriage, when it came, was a more equal partnership between husband and wife than it had ever been before. One inevitable consequence was a reduction in the frequency of childbearing.[79]

Since the Second World War, and especially since the 1960s, the effect on marital fertility of growing opportunities for employment among unmarried women has been reinforced by a revolutionary increase in the extent of employment among married women, itself a product of the relatively rapid recent growth of the service sector of the economy. This produced a range of occupations and occupational environments so much more congenial to women than the physically

arduous, repetitive, dirty and largely manufacturing work hitherto available that even married women, who usually have
less need to seek employment than single women, were increasingly willing to forego childbirth in order to benefit from
the additional income, independence and self-esteem they
permitted.[80] Given that much of the modern decline in fertility had already been accomplished by the time married
women first became extensively employed outside the home,
the rise in labour participation ratios among married females
was clearly less significant for the fertility transition than the
growth of employment opportunities for unmarried females.
Probably, too, neither influence was as important as the contribution made by the effect of economic modernisation on
the nature of the family economy and, in particular, on the
position of children within it.[81]

Three aspects of the changes which have occurred in the
economic role of the family have been especially critical in
reducing levels of marital fertility. The first was the transfer of
support for elderly, infirm or unemployed parents from children to the state or private, commercial organisations, a transfer made possible by an unprecedented rise in levels of
personal and community wealth. Even if this argument somewhat exaggerates the extent of the support provided by children in earlier times, there is no doubt that the emergence of
alternative sources of succour for parents in crisis or old age
has helped to undermine the necessity for high fertility
norms.[82] More crucial to an understanding of the causes of
the fertility transition, however, were two other changes in the
nature of the family economy: the replacement of the family
by large-scale, capitalist institutions as the principal producer
of material goods; and the requirements of increasingly
sophisticated forms of business organisation and technology
for an ever more highly educated and competitively selected
labour force.

In traditional economies, where the family was the main
supplier of goods and most productive processes had little
need for highly trained and formally educated labour, even if
the net returns to children were slighter and less prolonged

than is sometimes supposed, large numbers of offspring were an economic asset. Because children made a substantial contribution to family income and required little in the way of expenditure on training and education in return, the distribution of family resources favoured the adult male family head and the elderly at the expense of the young and other dependants. The resulting upward flow of wealth meant that men dominated the decision-making process and, coupled with the belief that children were a valuable source of labour and security, ensured that fertility norms remained high.

In modern economies the function of the family, and thus the distribution of resources and authority within it, differs. Partly because of the need for a more educated workforce, selected in the interests of efficiency on the basis of educational attainment rather than personal patronage, and partly because of the introduction of legislation against child employment, children are a net financial burden. At least until the second half of the twentieth century, when the employment of married women outside the home first reached significant levels, the result was a steady increase in the share of total family income contributed by the adult male breadwinner and a redistribution of family resources in favour of children. This gave husbands as well as wives a powerful incentive to limit fertility. Simultaneously, the authority of parents over their offspring was being eroded by the spread of formal systems of education which undermined the claims of parents to greater knowledge and wisdom, replaced success in domestic chores by success in schoolwork as the principal determinant of status and advancement and encouraged among the young a sense of egalitarianism, individualism and rationality and levels of expectation that were often at odds with those of parents and grandparents. As children's respect for parental authority declined and children became more demanding in terms of what they expected parents to provide, the emotional strains of parenthood intensified. On emotional as much as financial grounds having fewer children made sense.[83] Of course, since childrearing itself in many respects became easier in the course of economic modernisation, lower rates of fertility were only acceptable if there existed attractive alternatives to children that would otherwise have had to be foregone. It is no coincidence that only in the last hundred years or so, as a result of the higher incomes, more congenial employment opportunities and proliferation of consumer goods and leisure facilities made possible by economic modernisation, have such alternatives become available for sufficient numbers of people to permit reductions in fertility in all socio-occupational groups.[84]

Recently the search for a satisfactory explanation of the modern fertility transition has switched its emphasis from economic to ideational influences. Some scholars, it is true, maintain that changes in the latter are merely functions of changes in the former and should therefore be regarded as of only secondary importance.[85] Others, however, insist that ideational changes, at least in part, occur independently of economic forces.[86] Whichever view is the correct one, the contribution of ideational impulses to the long-term decline in marital fertility obviously deserves close scrutiny.

According to the ideationalist interpretation, changes in fertility schedules are more a response to changes in attitudes, motives and ideals than to changes in the structure of demographic, economic or technological systems. Ideational change, it is argued, facilitated fertility decline in two ways: first by encouraging attitudes more sympathetic to the use of birth control procedures and more inclined to regard birth control as beneficial; second by altering the definition of good fatherhood and motherhood in ways that persuaded fathers to become more aware of the burdens imposed on women by excessive childbearing, more involved in domestic duties and more willing to treat marriage as a partnership of equals, and mothers to measure success more in terms of the quality than the quantity of the children they bore. Prompted by the work of health visitors, infant welfare centres, school medical inspectors and care committees, the argument goes, from the early years of the twentieth century relationships between husbands and wives and perceptions of parenthood were redefined in ways inimical to frequent childbearing.[87]

111

Of all the changes that have occurred in western ideational systems in recent centuries two are considered especially critical to the adoption of lower fertility norms. The first was the trend away from beliefs which regarded procreation as the sole purpose of sexual intercourse and the environment as largely unalterable, towards more secularist, less fatalistic beliefs which encouraged sexual activity for reasons of affection or pleasure, and the notion that the environment was controllable, problems solvable and progress possible. The second was the emergence of a philosophy of individualism which freed the individual from communal and family control, thereby increasing his freedom of choice and action and fostering the pursuit of self-interest, self-respect and self-improvement. To a large extent these changes were a consequence of economic modernisation and the materialist values and aspirations which, particularly from the later decades of the nineteenth century, emerged with it. But they also owed something to the philosophers of the eighteenth-century intellectual enlightenment whose concern for the rights of the individual nourished both criticism of traditional customs and institutions, and the rise of new ideals of liberty and democracy. Together the forces of secularism, rationalism and individualism, complemented by rising standards of education, helped to raise the status of women and children to levels incompatible with the maintenance of high fertility rates.[88]

No one would dispute the truth of Chesnais' claim that explanations of the modern fertility transition must incorporate more than just economic factors. By themselves material circumstances cannot entirely account for what has happened to fertility norms since the late nineteenth century.[89] Some scholars continue to stress the primacy of economic determinants.[90] Others, more impressed by the apparently closer relationship between fertility and cultural, ethnic and linguistic traits than between fertility and economic circumstances, and by the great variety of economic environments within which the fertility transition occurred, prefer to emphasise the role of ideational systems, particularly during the initial stages of the transition.[91] All, however, are agreed that the causes of fertility decline were complex and multilayered. Clearly, some of the most important originated, directly or indirectly, in the process of modern economic growth; lower rates of infant and child mortality; higher real incomes and a wider range of attractive alternatives to children; increased employment opportunities for women; higher child costs; more generous state support for the elderly, infirm and unemployed; increased rates of migration which helped overcome regional cultural barriers to the spread of the small family ideal; and the impact on attitudes to family size of higher standards of material well-being in childhood which impelled future parents to sacrifice excessive childbearing in the interests of maintaining a standard of life they were reluctant to lose.[92] No less important, however, was the influence of more secular and individualistic mentalities and patterns of behaviour which, in part anyway, emerged independently of the process of economic modernisation.

In short, the modern fertility transition had no single cause nor even a single set of causes. Its determinants were so numerous, their mix so varied by time, class and place and their influence so difficult to quantify that many scholars feel it may never be possible to provide an accurate weighting of the relative importance of each of the agents involved, let alone an agreed, overall explanatory model of the phenomenon.[93]

The factors responsible for the variations which have occurred in levels of marital fertility since the Second World War are equally complex and difficult to unravel. Here too the similarities of experience between Britain and other developed countries strongly imply the operation of a common factor or common mix of factors.[94] But what this was has also still to be finally determined.

It is generally agreed that changes in levels of infant and child mortality were of little relevance. While the continued decline of infant and child death rates may have contributed something to the re-emergence of declining levels of marital fertility from the mid 1960s, the rise in marital fertility in the decade or so prior to the mid 1960s occurred at a time of falling, not rising, infant and death rates. The sequence of baby boom and baby bust which was shared by all developed countries in the third quarter of the twentieth century cannot easily be explained by reference to trends in survival rates during the earliest years of life.

Of greater significance was the legalisation of abortion and developments in the technology of birth control. Before the 1967 Abortion Act, which became effective in April 1968 and greatly extended the criteria under which terminations were permitted by law, abortion was legally permissible only when the life of the mother was thought to be at risk. The impact of the Act on abortion rates was spectacular. In England and Wales the number of legal abortions per thousand women aged 15–44 soared from 3.5 in 1968 to 11.4 in 1973. By 1976 it had fallen to 10.5. Thereafter, except in 1983 when there was a slight decline, it rose in each successive year to 15.5 by 1989, a level equivalent to about one abortion for every five recorded conceptions.[95]

In the absence of data on the frequency of illegal abortion it is unclear how much responsibility to attach to the legalisation of abortion for trends in marital fertility from the mid 1960s. Probably its contribution was limited. For one thing the culmination of the baby boom clearly long predated the implementation of the 1967 Act. For another the adoption of more liberal abortion laws was itself a consequence of the forces of economic and ideational change and therefore should not be accorded too independent or significant a role. Thirdly, however much the liberalisation of abortion legislation contributed to the downturn in marital fertility between the late 1960s and late 1970s, it was obviously of little relevance in the 1980s when, despite persistent increases in abortion ratios, fertility rates either stabilised or rose. As Coleman and Salt conclude, the introduction of legalised abortion probably accounted for no more than a fifth of the overall decline in levels of legitimate fertility after 1967–8.[96]

Until the mid 1960s the most common forms of contraception were withdrawal and the use of condoms and chemical spermicides. A female contraceptive pill first became widely available in the early 1960s and by the mid 1970s was the single most popular method of birth control. Among other birth control technologies to have grown in popularity since the 1960s are the intrauterine device and sterilisation. After 1976, as a result of the pill scares of 1970–2 and 1977–8 when higher than anticipated mortality among women using oral contraceptives encouraged those over 30 to switch to alternative methods, reliance on the pill declined and sterilisation, in particular, became increasingly common.

Before 1968 access to the contraceptive services offered by the National Health Service was restricted solely to women with proven medical reasons for avoiding pregnancy. Subsequently, under the terms of the 1967 Family Planning Act, local authorities were empowered, though not obliged, to supply contraceptives and contraceptive advice on social as well as medical grounds, and in practice most did so. From 1972 these powers included the provision of vasectomies for men and, from 1974, sterilisation for women. Beginning in 1974, in the case of contraceptives prescribed and dispensed through local authority NHS clincs, and in 1975, in the case of those supplied by general practitioners, contraceptive services were made available free of charge.[97]

If only because periods of rising or stable rates of fertility from the mid 1950s to mid 1960s and late 1970s to late 1980s were also periods of advance in the extent and efficiency of birth control practices, it is obvious that variations in the incidence and effectiveness of contraception cannot be given the primary responsibility for shaping postwar marital fertility trends. In any case, rates of fertility within marriage had already fallen to very low levels long before the widespread adoption of devices such as the pill, the coil and sterilisation, while similarly low rates of fertility within marriage were also achieved in countries where the most sophisticated methods of birth control were practised much less extensively than in Britain.[98]

Even so, the fact that the reappearance of fertility decline between the mid 1960s and late 1970s coincided with a period of abnormally rapid progress in the availability and application of more efficient, lower cost and easier to use contraceptives suggests that, during this period of least, improved birth control technologies did make some contribution to the reduction in family size.

In this context it is often argued that the female contraceptive pill played a particularly important role. Improvements in birth control methods, it has been suggested, may help to explain why Roman Catholics, whose fertility declined especially rapidly, increasingly denied a value system which discouraged all 'artificial' forms of family limitation.[99] According to Ni Bhrolchain, the greater ability of improved birth control devices to prevent unwanted pregnancies also helps to explain why the growth of female employment between the mid 1950s and early 1960s was accompanied by rising fertility, while its continued growth in the later 1960s and 1970s was accompanied by falling fertility.[100] Murphy goes even further. In his view the female contraceptive pill, adopted not in response to the forces of socio-economic or ideational change but simply because it was a more effective means of avoiding pregnancy than any previously available, was the *principal* determinant of British marital fertility trends between the mid 1960s and late 1970s. Significantly, Murphy claims, when concern over the health-risks of the pill in the early and late 1970s led to reductions in its use, the switch to less reliable methods of contraception was followed by a temporary increase in the number of conceptions.[101]

Yet, even for the period between the mid 1960s and late 1970s when the relationship between improved methods of contraception and falling rates of fertility appears strongest, the case for interpreting fertility trends in terms of changes in the nature of birth control technology should not be pressed too far. Fundamental to its validity is the assumption that the baby bust was a consequence not of a reduction in the number of children *desired* but of the success of improved contraception in reducing the number of *unwanted* conceptions. The flaw in this assumption is that decreasing numbers of unwanted pregnancies accounted for only a small part of the overall drop in fertility between the mid 1960s and late 1970s. Fertility fell because couples wanted fewer children, not because better contraceptive technology made it easier to avoid overshooting fertility targets which were as low during the period of the baby boom as during the period of the baby bust. Undue emphasis on the contribution of the pill also sits uncomfortably with the fact that a similar decline in fertility occurred in other European countries where the pill was not extensively used. Furthermore, although the temporary upturn in fertility in 1971 correlated reasonably neatly with the pill scare of 1970–2 and may well have been caused by it, fertility had already begun to rise before the second pill scare of 1977–8 and must have originated in factors other than a switch to less effective methods of contraception. While allowing new birth control technology some part in initiating the collapse of the late 1950s and early 1960s baby boom, it is surely more appropriate to regard this technology more as a means than a basic cause of the further decline in levels of marital fertility which began in the second half of the 1960s. In the main it is to changes in socio-economic and ideational circumstances that we should turn for an explanation of postwar fertility fluctuations.[102]

To some extent, it has been suggested, variations in levels of marital fertility after the Second World War were simply the result of variations in levels of general prosperity. In conditions like those of Britain before the mid 1960s, where few married women were employed outside the home, rates of fertility (and nuptiality) were partly a direct function of trends in the earning capacity of men. During the years of severe economic depression between the world wars, when levels of unemployment were high, housing relatively expensive and difficult to obtain, and male real wages much lower than they were subsequently to be, rates of marital fertility fell.[103] Once the brief postwar surge in marriage and fertility was completed, economic austerity and housing shortages in the late 1940s and early 1950s combined to reduce fertility rates to levels no higher than in the 1930s. In the decade or so beginning around the mid 1950s, by contrast, the pace of economic growth accelerated, unemployment largely disappeared, male real incomes soared and, thanks to extensive public and private sector building programmes, the problem of housing shortage was considerably alleviated. The result, achieved primarily through an increase in the numbers of first and second births, was an unexpected boom in marital fertility. The boom was intensified by the fact that economic depression in the interwar period, together with the demands made on resources by the needs of war and postwar industrial reconstruction, greatly reduced the standard of living expectations of consumers throughout the 1950s and early 1960s. Because this coincided with a period of dramatic improvement in the real wages of men, it widened the gap between incomes and expectations and thus increased the surplus available for spending on additional children. Frequent contemporary comparisons between the performance of the economy before and after the mid 1950s added another powerful, psychological impulse in favour of higher fertility. After the mid 1960s, the argument continues, declining rates of economic growth, increasing economic instability and rising levels of unemployment and inflation, coupled with the effect of higher standard of living expectations created during the years of prosperity in the 1950s and early 1960s, worked to force fertility down.[104]

For the period before the mid 1960s the association between periods of low fertility and low incomes–high unemployment, and periods of high fertility and high incomes–low unemployment is sufficiently regular to support the belief that temporal trends in levels of fertility were at least partly a direct response to variations in rates of economic growth. Since the mid 1960s, however, the nature of the relationship between fertility and economic growth has changed from positive to negative: whenever real incomes have risen and unemployment fallen, rates of marital fertility have decreased, not increased. Thus, rising per capita real incomes between 1970 and 1976 were accompanied by a decline in fertility, and falling real incomes in 1977 by a rise in fertility between 1978 and 1980. In most recent times, it seems, periods of rising income have increased the attractions of alternatives to childbearing and discouraged rather than encouraged conception.[105] A similar change took place in the nature of the relationship between fertility and housing. In contrast to the experience of earlier periods when levels of fertility correlated positively with the availability of housing, the decline in fertility after the mid 1960s occurred against a background of improving, not deteriorating, housing provision.[106]

The absence of a positive correlation between rates of fertility and rates of economic growth in the period since the mid 1960s has led some scholars to suggest that a more convincing explanation of postwar fertility trends lies in the changes which have occurred in the relationship between the incomes of parents and their children.

The explanation has been presented in two forms. The first, developed by Easterlin, sees the evolution of marital fertility chiefly as a result of changes in the relationship between the earnings and standard of living expectations of young adults of childbearing age, on the one hand, and the earnings of their fathers, on the other. If, on entering adulthood, the earnings of sons relative to those of their fathers are high, standard of living expectations fashioned in childhood and adolescence will be relatively easy to attain and fertility will rise. If, however, a son's earnings are low relative to those of the father, expectations established in childhood will be higher and more difficult to attain and fertility will decline in order to satisfy them.[107] In the alternative variant, developed by Oppenheimer, the 'relative income' (or 'relative economic status') of adult sons is determined not only by their earnings relative to those of their fathers, but also relative both to those of their mothers and to the size of the family in which sons spent their childhood and adolescence. Generally, the income and standard of living aspirations of adult sons compared to those of their parents varies inversely with the size of their birth cohort. For sons born during periods of low fertility, early adulthood is associated with abundant opportunities for education, employment and advancement and incomes sufficient to permit high fertility without sacrificing their material expectations. Sons born during periods of high fertility, on the other hand, face greater competition for work and training when they reach adulthood. Compared with those of their parents, earnings and prospects will be poor, and fertility has to be reduced to allow standard of living aspirations to be achieved. Thus, the argument goes, for children born during the low fertility decade of the 1930s and entering the labour market in the prosperous 1950s and early 1960s 'relative incomes' were sufficiently high to provoke a boom in births; for children born during the higher fertility era of the 1950s and early 1960s, who entered the more depressed and crowded labour markets of the 1970s and early 1980s, standard of living aspirations were harder to attain and baby boom accordingly gave way to baby bust.[108]

Empirical tests of the Easterlin–Oppenheimer variants of the 'relative income' interpretation of twentieth-century marital fertility trends have yielded mixed results. In the case of Germany the significance of the Easterlin variant has been described as 'weak', and even for the United States, for which it was initially devised, recent studies have failed to confirm its claims.[109] In the case of Britain, it seems to have some validity in the period down to the mid 1960s, when married women contributed little to family income, but not thereafter, when married women's contribution to family income increased. According to Crafts, trends in 'relative income' (as defined by Easterlin) go a long way towards explaining the decline in rates of fertility in England and Wales between 1877 and 1937.[110] As the Easterlin thesis predicts, rising levels of fertility in Britain between 1955 and 1964 coincided with, and were partly caused by, higher incomes relative to standard of living expectations among adult sons than among their fathers. Yet, as indicated by the lack of an obvious relationship between variations in fertility and 'relative income' during the years 1961–4, even within the period 1955–64 the correlation between the two variables was not always close. After the mid 1960s it almost entirely disappeared. Whereas fertility rates began to fall from 1964, the 'relative incomes' of childbearing age groups continued to rise into 1965–6. And, while declining rates of fertility coincided with declining 'relative incomes' in the later 1960s, the quickening pace of fertility decline in the 1970s occurred against a background of markedly

120

improving 'relative incomes' among young adult males. At best, it seems, the Easterlin model is of only limited value as an explanation of postwar British marital fertility trends.[111]

Oppenheimer's variant of the 'relative income' hypothesis, in which rising levels of employment among mothers aged 35–44 in the 1950s and early 1960s increased standard of living expectations and thus depressed the 'relative income' of their adult children, has generally been considered a more satisfactory explanation for the downturn in fertility rates in the second half of the 1960s and 1970s. However, as Ermisch points out, its appeal owes much to the fact that it is difficult to subject to rigorous empirical testing. In the real world the effect of increasing female employment on the 'relative income' of children is especially difficult to quantify. Whether or not 'relative income' (as defined by Oppenheimer) did decline after 1964 remains unclear.[112] Supporters of the Oppenheimer interpretation can take little comfort from the findings of a recent analysis of the relationship between fertility and cohort size in 16 European countries since 1950 which shows that, with the *possible* and at best only partial exceptions of Belgium, England and Wales, Finland, France and Italy, temporal trends in rates of fertility have not been dominated by the workings of the 'relative income' variable.[113] No less disturbing is the fact that cohort studies carried out for Britain as a whole show a positive, not negative, correlation between a woman's fertility and the size of the family in which she grew up.[114] The implication is that neither the Easterlin nor the Oppenheimer variants of the 'relative income' hypothesis can safely be regarded as adequate explanations of fertility trends since the Second World War.

Of all the suggested explanations of postwar variations in marital fertility, the one currently seen as best fitting the pattern of boom and bust is the 'New Home Economics' thesis. This argues that the evolution of fertility in Britain and other developed countries in recent times has been determined primarily by changes in the proportions of married women employed outside the home, and thus in the ratios of women's to men's wages. The thesis is based on the premise that attitudes to procreation differ from household to household according to whether or not the woman is gainfully employed. In households where the man is the sole breadwinner rising real incomes lead to an increase in fertility. In households where both partners are employed, growing opportunities for female employment and increases in the ratio of female to male earnings encourage women to seek work and, by raising the opportunity costs of time of children, reduce fertility.[115]

Initially conceived for the United States, the 'New Home Economics' model has received widespread support as an explanation of postwar British marital fertility trends. Partly as a result of the growth of non-manual, service occupations after the mid 1960s, and partly in response to the passing of an Equal Pay Act in 1970, which required that women receive the same rate of pay as men for the same job and thus helped to raise the ratio of female to male wages from under two-thirds in the 1960s to around three-quarters by the mid 1970s, the proportion of economically active women in the age groups 20–64 rose from about one-third throughout the first half of the century to 42 per cent by 1961, 52 per cent by 1971, and 61 per cent by 1981.[116] On the eve of the First World War and throughout the interwar period fewer than one in ten married women were employed outside the home. By the mid 1960s the figure had risen to nearly four in ten and by the late 1980s to six in ten.[117] One authority has estimated that for a cross-section of British mothers in 1980 the income that would have been lost by having children amounted to as much as 43 per cent of a mother's lifetime earnings.[118]

The consequences for marital fertility, it is claimed, were unmistakable. Throughout the 1950s and early 1960s levels of employment among married women and the ratio of female to male earnings were not yet high enough to offset the effect of rising male real incomes and, as a result, rates of marital fertility increased. After the mid 1960s they were, with the result that first births were increasingly postponed, childbearing became increasingly concentrated on women in their late twenties and early thirties, and overall levels of fertility within marriage declined.[119] But for the increase in the ratio of female to male wages which followed the implementation of the Equal Pay Act the number of births registered in England and Wales between 1975 and 1978 may well have been as much as 8 per cent higher than it was.[120] When in the late 1970s the ratio of female to male wages and the percentage of families in which both partners were employed temporarily declined, fertility rates once more began to rise.[121] The fact that variations in the extent of female employment are also known to have been a significant determinant of regional and socio-occupational class differentials in fertility may be taken as further testimony to the validity of the 'New Home Economics' model.[122]

Precisely which aspect of this model exercised the greatest influence on fertility rates has still to be finally resolved. Arguably, rising levels of female employment *per se* were less important than other facets of the female work experience. Contrary to what the model predicts, low rates of fertility in postwar Japan coincided with unusually low, not high, ratios of married women in employment.[123] In Britain rates of marital fertility among upper-class females changed little after the Second World War despite a considerable increase in their labour participation ratios, while the fertility of working-class females, whose participation in gainful employment remained relatively constant, decreased.[124]

More important, perhaps, were the effects of changes which occurred in the timing of married women's employment. By encouraging women to shorten their birth intervals and increase the tempo of childbearing in the early years of married life, growing opportunities for female employment during the 1950s and early 1960s worked to raise overall levels of marital fertility.[125] By the 1970s, because they were now accompanied by a new tendency for married women to return to work between births, improved job prospects for females acted to lengthen birth intervals and thus to reduce aggregate marital fertility rates.

But the aspect of the 'New Home Economics' interpretation which probably exerted the greatest influence on marital fertility, at least in the 1970s, was the sudden and pronounced improvement which occurred in the ratio of female to male earnings following the 1970 Equal Pay Act. This alone goes a long way towards explaining why rates of fertility in Britain fell by 26 per cent between 1970 and 1975, compared with a fall of just 16 per cent between 1965 and 1970 and a *rise* of 6 per cent between 1976 and 1981.[126]

To interpret variations in levels of marital fertility in the second half of the twentieth century solely in economic terms, however, is unwise and misleading. The baby boom of the mid 1950s to mid 1960s, for example, was due to much more than the influence of economic forces alone. In part it also owed something to the fact that the men and women who were then of reproductive age retained some of the mentalities of an earlier value system which favoured higher fertility norms. In part it was the understandable reaction of a generation that had lived through the traumas of war and for which the attractions of a secure and full family life were particularly appealing. In part too it reflected the emergence of a more sympathetic attitude towards children, itself a combined result of wartime propaganda emphasising the importance of woman's role as mother and sexual comforter of man, growing concern over the potential economic and political dangers thought to be inherent in low rates of population growth, and the introduction of government initiatives to strengthen family values and reduce the costs of childrearing in response to this concern.

The subsequent baby bust likewise owed much to non-economic influences. Children born between the mid 1940s and mid 1960s, and especially those born in the prosperous 1950s and early 1960s, avoided the disappointments and traumas suffered by their parents and were therefore inclined to regard high fertility less sympathetically. In this they were encouraged by a radical re-evaluation of the population problem, which substituted a concern for too few people with a concern for too many people. Coupled with advances in education and science which further eroded traditional rationales for high fertility and the political uncertainties provoked by the Cold War and conflicts in Vietnam and elsewhere, attitudinal changes of this type contributed significantly to the downturn in fertility rates from the mid 1960s.

Fundamental to them all, however, was an accelerating transformation of values away from a primary concern with the interests of collective 'institutions' such as kinship networks, the church, the community and the state, which favoured high fertility, towards a primary concern with the interests of the individual, which favoured low fertility. When, as in the twenty years or so immediately following the Second World War, collective and individual interests happened to coincide, rates of marital fertility rose. When, as has increasingly been the case since the mid 1960s, these interests conflicted, rates of marital fertility declined. Under the impact of a value system which gave so much encouragement to ambitions for self-fulfilment and self-improvement it was inevitable that more importance would be attached to the quality than the quantity of children and that rates of fertility would once again start to decline.[127] When its ideational determinants are added to its economic determinants, it is clear that the causes of short-term variations in levels of marital fertility during the second half of the twentieth century are just as intricate and difficult to quantify as the factors responsible for the permanent reduction in marital fertility targets which began in the later decades of the nineteenth century.[128]

CONCLUSION

Perhaps because of the greater challenges afforded by the relative paucity of its source-materials and the partial and at times dubious reliability of the raw demographic data these yield, historians of population have always shown more interest in the demography of the more distant than the more recent past.

By improving our understanding of earlier trends in rates of population growth and the mechanisms of fertility, mortality and migration that were responsible for them, this preference has made it possible to better appreciate the dramatic nature of the changes which have occurred in demographic systems during the last hundred years or so. This is not, of course, to deny the existence of significant demographic changes in earlier times. The period between the late eighteenth and late nineteenth centuries, for instance, was characterised by wholly unprecedented innovations in rates of population increase, patterns of internal migration and residential distribution and levels of overseas migration. And, as we have seen, some of what were to become established features of twentieth-century demography – among them the persistence of high volumes of emigration and immigration and of net losses on balance of international migration, the decline in fertility and the rise in life expectancy – had already begun to emerge in the late nineteenth century, or in some cases even earlier. Generally, however, the startling differences between the demographic environments of present day and late eighteenth-century Britain, outlined and analysed in this book, were a twentieth-century creation.

If the word 'revolutionary' can ever safely be applied to phases of population history, it is surely more appropriate to apply it to the period after rather than before the turn into our own century. Low and declining rates of population growth after the First World War were not in themselves a new phenomenon, but the fact that they were caused by falling fertility rather than rising mortality certainly was. Twentieth-century migrational and residential patterns favouring the south over the north, peripheral at the expense of core regions and smaller rather than larger communities, in nature if not in degree and causation reminiscent of pre-industrial times, differed fundamentally from the patterns of mobility and population location which prevailed throughout the later eighteenth and nineteenth centuries. The decline in rates of fertility and mortality, though already underway in the late nineteenth century, was likewise overwhelmingly a twentieth-century phenomenon, while levels of divorce, remarriage, extramarital cohabitation and illegitimacy in the later decades of the century reached heights unparalleled among previous generations. In these and numerous other respects the demography of Britain in the present century contrasts starkly with that of even the immediately preceding centuries.

It would be surprising, indeed, if it did not. Essentially, though not of course entirely, demographic systems are a function of the character of the economic environment within which they exist, and of the cultural, social and political circumstances which this environment helps to create. Until well into the second half of the nineteenth century the impact of the Industrial Revolution on the technology, scale and composition of economic activity, and thus on the demography of the society, was relatively muted. Beginning in the late nineteenth century the pace of technological and economic change accelerated dramatically. Inevitably this was accompanied by the emergence of a demographic system radically different from that which had persisted more or less unaltered in its broad fundamentals for centuries.

NOTES

1   POPULATION GROWTH AND LOCATION

1. E. A. Wrigley and R. S. Schofield, *The Population History of England, 1541–1871. A Reconstruction* (London, 1981), pp. 531–4.
2. The exceptions include Finland, Iceland, Northern Ireland, Portugal and the Irish Republic.
3. For example in Belgium, Denmark, Germany, Italy, Luxembourg, Sweden and the Irish Republic.
4. M. W. Flinn (ed.), *Scottish Population History from the Seventeenth Century to the 1930s* (Cambridge, 1977), p. 306.
5. R. Lawton, 'Population Changes in England and Wales in the Later Nineteenth Century: An Analysis of Trends by Registration Districts', *Transactions of the Institute of British Geographers*, XLIV (1968), 57, 62, 65. R. Lawton, 'Regional Population Trends in England and Wales, 1750–1971', in J. Hobcraft and P. Rees (eds), *Regional Demographic Development* (London, 1978), 32–3, 36–8, 40, 46, 52. D. Coleman and J. Salt, *The British Population, Patterns, Trends and Processes* (Oxford, 1992), p. 94.
6. A. G. Champion, 'Population Trends in the 1970s', in J. B. Goddard and A. G. Champion (eds), *The Urban and Regional Transformation of Britain* (London, 1983), p. 200.
7. S. Kennett and N. Spence, 'British Population Trends in the 1970s', *Town and Country Planning*, 48 (1979), 223. W. Randolph and S. Robert, 'Population Redistribution in Great Britain,

128

1971–81', *Town and Country Planning*, 50 (1981), 227. S. Robert and W. Randolph, 'Beyond Decentralization: the Evolution of Population Distribution in England and Wales, 1961–81', *Geoforum*, 14, 1 (1983), 81. Champion, 'Population Trends in the 1970s', 196–7, 200. A. G. Champion, 'Recent Changes in the Pace of Population Deconcentration in Britain', *Geoforum*, 18, 4 (1987), 383–6. M. Britton, 'Recent Population Changes in Perspective', *Population Trends*, 44 (1986), 34–5. Coleman and Salt, *The British Population*, p. 95. In the period 1971–4, when rates of population growth in the South East, South West and East Anglia barely exceeded those in the rest of Britain, the north–south drift of residence was temporarily halted. It re-emerged in the later 1970s. J. B. Goddard, 'Structural Change in the British Space Economy', in Goddard and Champion (eds), *Urban and Regional Transformation*, p. 15.

8. A. G. Champion, 'Population Trends in Rural Britain', *Population Trends*, 26 (1981), 22. Champion, 'Population Trends in the 1970s', 206. Champion, 'Recent Changes in the Pace of Population Deconcentration', 386. Coleman and Salt, *The British Population*, p. 89. Randolph and Robert, 'Population Redistribution', 228.

9. The region includes Argyll and Bute, Orkney, Shetlands and the Western Isles. Most of the growth was concentrated at Aviemore, Fort William, Invergordon and Inverness. H. Jones, J. Caird, W. Berry and J. Dewhurst, 'Peripheral Counter-Urbanization: Findings from an Integration of Census and Survey Data in Northern Scotland', *Regional Studies*, 20 (1986), 16.

10. Flinn (ed.), *Scottish Population History*, pp. 313–15.

11. Urban areas defined as settlements with a high degree of population density and a minimum of 2500 inhabitants. C. M. Law, 'The Growth of Urban Population in England and Wales 1801–1911', *Transactions of the Institute of British Geographers*, XLI (1967), 130. C. M. Law, 'Some Notes on the Urban Population of England and Wales in the 18th Century', *The Local Historian*, 10, 1 (1972), 18–19, 22. For details of the spatial evolution of urbanisation in England and Wales see D. Friedlander, 'The Spread of Urbanisation in England and Wales, 1851–1951', *Population Studies*, 24, 3 (1970), 422–43.

12. OPCS, Registrar-General Scotland, *Census 1981. Key Statistics for Urban Areas. Great Britain. Cities and Towns* (London, 1984), pp. 107–8.

13. From data in B. R. Mitchell with P. Deane, *Abstract of British Historical Statistics* (Cambridge, 1962), pp. 24–7.

14. S. R. Kennett, 'Migration Within and Between Labour Markets', in Goddard and Champion (eds), *Urban and Regional Transformation*, p. 217. Champion, 'Population Trends in the 1970s', 189. A. G. Champion, 'United Kingdom: Population Deconcentration as a Cyclic Phenomenon', in A. G. Champion (ed.), *Counterurbanization: The Changing Pace and Nature of Population Deconcentration* (London, 1989), pp. 83, 88, 90. Coleman and Salt, *The British Population*, p. 96.

15. Randolph and Robert, 'Population Redistribution', 88. Champion, 'United Kingdom', 89–90.

16. During the 1960s the population of Liverpool fell by over 18 per cent, of Manchester and Newcastle by over 17 per cent and of Birmingham by over 8 per cent, losses that were between two and three times greater than in the 1950s. Champion, 'Population Trends in the 1970s', 189.

17. Champion, 'Population Trends in the 1970s', 190. Kennett, 'Migration Within and Between Labour Markets', 217.

18. Coleman and Salt, *The British Population*, p. 99.

19. Robert and Randolph, 'Beyond Decentralization', 79, 90.

20. Principal cities – Birmingham, Leeds, Liverpool, London, Manchester, Sheffield. Large cities – Bristol, Cardiff, Derby, Hull, Leicester, Nottingham, Plymouth, Southampton, Stoke, Swansea. Small cities – Bath, Brighton, Cambridge, Cheltenham, Durham, Exeter, Gloucester, Lincoln, Middlesborough, Newport, Norwich, Oxford, Preston, Reading, York, Worcester. Coleman and Salt, *The British Population*, pp. 96, 102, 104. Robert and Randolph, 'Beyond Decentralization', 76, 80. Kennett and Spence, 'British Population Trends in the 1970s', 221. Kennett, 'Migration Within and Between Labour Markets', 217, 219, 221.

21. Coleman and Salt, *The British Population*, p. 105. Champion, 'United Kingdom', 91.

22. Kennett and Spence, 'British Population Trends in the 1970s', 222–3. Randolph and Robert, 'Population Redistribution', 228. Robert and Randolph, 'Beyond Decentralization', 83. Champion, 'Population Trends in the 1970s', 194, 204. Britton, 'Recent Population Changes in Perspective', 33, 35–8. Champion, 'Recent Changes in the Pace of Population Deconcentration', 379, 381, 389, 391. A. G. Champion and P. D. Congdon, 'An Analysis of the Recovery of Greater London's Population Change Rate', *Built Environment*, 13 (1988), 193–211. Champion, 'United Kingdom', 83, 90. A. G.

Champion, 'Introduction: The Counterurbanization Experience', in Champion (ed.), *Counterurbanization*, 13. Coleman and Salt, *The British Population*, pp. 83, 105, 107.

23. Randolph and Robert, 'Population Redistribution', 227–8. Robert and Randolph, 'Beyond Decentralization', 83. Britton, 'Recent Population Changes in Perspective', 38. Champion, 'Recent Changes in the Pace of Population Deconcentration', 386–7. Champion, 'United Kingdom', 92. C. Jones and Bob Armitage, 'Population Changes within Area Types: England and Wales, 1971–88', *Population Trends*, 60 (1990), 28. Coleman and Salt, *The British Population*, p. 107. Between 1971 and 1981 the population of inner London fell almost 18 per cent and that of outer London by 5 per cent: between 1981 and 1991 by 6 per cent and 4 per cent respectively. OPCS, *1991 Census. Preliminary Report for England and Wales* (London, 1991), p. 6.

24. See data in Robert and Randolph, 'Beyond Decentralization', 89–90.

25. Robert and Randolph, 'Beyond Decentralization', 82–3, 88–9. Champion, 'Population Trends in the 1970s', 208. Champion, 'Recent Changes in the Pace of Population Deconcentration', 391. Champion, 'Introduction: the Counterurbanization Experience', 13. Champion, 'United Kingdom', 87, 90–2. Coleman and Salt, *The British Population*, p. 105.

26. OPCS, *1991 Census*, pp. 5–6. See also Champion, 'Introduction: the Counterurbanization Experience', 13. Jones and Armitage, 'Population Changes within Area Types', 28, 30. Coleman and Salt, *The British Population*, pp. 105, 107.

27. Champion, 'Recent Changes in the Pace of Population Deconcentration', 386–7. See also Britton, 'Recent Population Changes in Perspective', 33, 38, 41.

28. Robert and Randolph, 'Beyond Decentralization', 79. Champion, 'Recent Changes in the Pace of Population Deconcentration', 388, 391. Champion, 'United Kingdom', 93. Jones and Armitage, 'Population Changes within Area Types', 27, 32.

29. Champion, 'Population Trends in Rural Britain', 20. Robert and Randolph, 'Beyond Decentralization', 76–9. Champion, 'Recent Changes in the Pace of Population Deconcentration', 379. Champion, 'Introduction: the Counterurbanization Experience', 1, 3–9, 11–13, 15–16. A. G. Champion, 'Conclusion: Temporary Anomaly, Long-Term Trend or Transitional Phase?', in Champion (ed.), *Counterurbanization*, pp. 230–3.

2 INTERNAL AND OVERSEAS MIGRATION

1. Wrigley and Schofield, *The Population History of England*, pp. 227–8.
2. See also Lawton, 'Regional Population Trends in England and Wales', 30, 48. Champion, 'Population Trends in the 1970s', 197–8. Britton, 'Recent Population Changes in Perspective', 33–5. Jones and Armitage, 'Population Changes within Area Types', 25.
3. Flinn (ed.), *Scottish Population History*, pp. 441–4, 446. See also Champion, 'Population Trends in the 1970s', 197–8. Registrar-General Scotland, *Annual Report 1980* (Edinburgh 1982), p. 281. Registrar-General Scotland, *Annual Report 1990* (Edinburgh, 1991), p. 109.
4. Flinn (ed.), *Scottish Population History*, p. 442. Registrar-General Scotland, *Annual Report 1990*, p. 107.
5. Flinn (ed.), *Scottish Population History*, pp. 461, 464–5.
6. H. R. Jones, J. B. Caird, W. G. Berry and N. J. Ford, 'Counterurbanization: English Migration to the Scottish Highlands and Islands', in H. Jones (ed.), *Population Change in Contemporary Scotland* (Norwich, 1984), pp. 73, 78. H. Jones, N. Ford, J. Caird and W. Berry, 'Counterurbanization in Societal Context: Long-Distance Migration to the Highlands and Islands of Scotland', *Professional Geographer*, 36 (1984), 438. Registrar-General Scotland, *Annual Report 1980*, pp. 281–3. Registrar-General Scotland, *Annual Report 1990*, p. 109.
7. Lawton, 'Regional Population Trends in England and Wales', 41, 45, 48, 61. In the case of the South East region the main mechanism of population growth changed between the 1950s and 1960s from migration to natural increase. See also Lawton, 'Population Changes in England and Wales in the Later Nineteenth Century', 60.
8. Jones and Armitage, 'Population Changes within Area Types', 29–30. Britton, 'Recent Population Changes in Perspective', 36. Champion, 'Recent Changes in the Pace of Population Deconcentration', 393–4. A. J. Fielding, 'Counterurbanization', in M. Pacione (ed.), *Population Geography: Progress and Prospect* (London, 1986), p. 226.
9. Lawton, 'Population Changes in England and Wales in the Later Nineteenth Century', 65. Lawton, 'Regional Population Trends in England and Wales', 46, 52, 56–7.
10. For examples see Robert and Randolph, 'Beyond Decentralization', 96. Champion, 'Population Trends in the

1970s', 198. Champion, 'Recent Changes in the Pace of Population Deconcentration', 392–3, 395. Jones and Armitage, 'Population Changes within Area Types', 38.

11. Robert and Randolph, 'Beyond Decentralization', 91–2. Champion, 'Population Trends in the 1970s', 198, 203. J. Stillwell, 'The Analysis and Projection of Interregional Migration in the United Kingdom', in R. Woods and P. Rees (eds), *Population Structures and Models. Developments in Spatial Demography* (London, 1986), p. 160. Champion, 'Recent Changes in the Pace of Population Deconcentration', 392–3, 395. Champion, 'United Kingdom', 93–4. Champion, 'Conclusion', 235. Jones and Armitage, 'Population Changes within Area Types', 28–30, 32. Coleman and Salt, *The British Population*, p. 411.

12. D. Baines, *Migration in a Mature Economy. Emigration and Internal Migration in England and Wales, 1861–1900* (Cambridge, 1985), pp. 49, 57, 300.

13. Mitchell with Deane, *Abstract of British Historical Statistics*, p. 47.

14. Baines, *Migration in a Mature Economy*, p. 57.

15. The number of Irish-born residents of mainland Britain rose from 20 000 in 1787 to 727 000 in 1851. J. G. Williamson, 'The Impact of the Irish on British Labour Markets During the Industrial Revolution', *Journal of Economic History*, XLVI, 3 (1986), 707.

16. Flinn (ed.), *Scottish Population History*, pp. 455, 457. C. Holmes, 'The Promised Land? Immigration into Britain, 1870–1980,' in D. A. Coleman (ed.), *Demography of Immigrants and Minority Groups in the United Kingdom* (London, 1982), pp. 5, 7. C. Holmes, 'The Impact of Immigration on British Society, 1870–1980', in T. Barker and M. Drake (eds), *Population and Society in Britain, 1850–1980* (London, 1982), p. 173. J. Walvin, *Passage to Britain. Immigration in British History and Politics* (Harmondsworth, 1984), p. 49. The number of Irish-born resident in England and Wales fell from 566 540 in 1871 to 375 325 in 1911. Walvin, *Passage to Britain*, pp. 61, 65.

17. Homes, 'The Promised Land?', 5, 7–8. Holmes, 'The Impact of Immigration', 173, 175. Walvin, *Passage to Britain*, pp. 62, 64, 68–9, 71–4. Flinn (ed.), *Scottish Population History*, pp. 455, 457–8.

18. Holmes, 'The Promised Land?', 6. Walvin, *Passage to Britain*, pp. 51, 82, 84–5. Coleman and Salt, *The British Population*, p. 455.

19. G. C. K. Peach, 'The Growth and Distribution of the Black Population in Britain, 1945–80', in Coleman (ed.), *Demography*

of Immigrants, pp. 26–8. Holmes, 'The Promised Land?', 3, 7. Holmes, 'The Impact of Immigration', 174. Walvin, *Passage to Britain*, pp. 97, 110, 117, 123. Coleman and Salt, *The British Population*, pp. 448–9, 451, 455, 464. I. Diamond and S. Clarke, 'Demographic Patterns Among Britain's Ethnic Groups', in H. Joshi (ed.), *The Changing Population of Britain* (Oxford, 1990), p. 179.

20. Walvin, *Passage to Britain*, pp. 105–6, 111–12. Holmes, 'The Promised Land?', 7. Holmes, 'The Impact of Immigration', 173–4. Coleman and Salt, *The British Population*, pp. 444–5, 455.

21. Diamond and Clarke, 'Demographic Patterns', 179.

22. J. Bailey, 'International Migration 1990', *Population Trends*, 67 (1992), 32.

23. Coleman and Salt, *The British Population*, pp. 442, 444. Diamond and Clarke, 'Demographic Patterns', 179. Holmes, 'The Promised Land?', 6–7.

24. The only exceptions were a few black Commonwealth seamen erroneously excluded by the 1925 Orders in Council. Holmes, 'The Promised Land?', 16.

25. The status of patrial was conferred by one or other of the following criteria: citizenship of self or parent or grandparent either by birth, adoption, registration or naturalisation in the United Kingdom: acceptance for settlement and residence in the United Kingdom for at least five years: Commonwealth citizens with a United Kingdom parent: spouses of patrials who were themselves Commonwealth citizens.

26. Holmes, 'The Promised Land?', 16. Holmes, 'The Impact of Immigration', 184–5. Walvin, *Passage to Britain*, pp. 66–7, 108–9, 117–21, 217. Diamond and Clarke, 'Demographic Patterns', 179. Peach, 'The Growth and Distribution', 30.

27. Walvin, *Passage to Britain*, pp. 66, 117–18. Coleman and Salt, *The British Population*, pp. 438–9. D. Feldman, 'The Importance of Being English. Jewish Immigration and the Decay of Liberal England', in D. Feldman and G. S. Jones (eds), *Metropolis London. Histories and Presentations Since 1800* (London, 1989), pp. 56, 58, 60.

28. Holmes, 'The Impact of Immigration', 175. Peach, 'The Growth and Distribution', 29–30. Walvin, *Passsage to Britain*, p. 111. Diamond and Clarke, 'Demographic Patterns', 178. Coleman and Salt, *The British Population*, pp. 439, 449, 451.

29. Peach, 'The Growth and Distribution', 27–8. Coleman and Salt, *The British Population*, p. 458. G. C. K. Peach, 'British Unemploy-

ment Cycles and West Indian Immigration, 1955–74', *New Community*, 7, (1978/9), 40–4.

30. Peach, 'The Growth and Distribution', 30, 34. See also Walvin, *Passage to Britain*, p. 108.

31. Holmes, 'The Promised Land?', 4—5. Walvin, *Passage to Britain*, pp. 110–12. Coleman and Salt, *The British Population*, p. 458.

32. Coleman and Salt, *The British Population*, p. 462. The continuing influence of pull factors is also attested by the fact that immigrant numbers were higher during the periods of relative economic prosperity in the 1960s and late 1980s than during the period of recession between the mid-1970s and mid-1980s.

33. Wrigley and Schofield, *The Population History of England*, pp. 219–22.

34. Between 1871 and 1931, 39 per cent of Scotland's total net emigration went to other parts of the United Kingdom and 61 per cent to overseas destinations. Flinn, *Scottish Population History*, pp. 441–2. Between 1931 and 1951 the share going overseas fell to under 5 per cent. In subsequent decades, as economic opportunities overseas improved relative to those in the United Kingdom, it rose, to 50 per cent in 1951–61, 48 per cent in 1961–71, 66 per cent in 1971–81 and 55 per cent in 1981–91.

35. J. -C. Chesnais, *The Demographic Transition. Stages, Patterns and Economic Implications* (Oxford, 1992), pp. 178–9.

36. D. S. Massey, 'Economic Development and International Migration in Comparative Perspective', *Population and Development Review*, 14, 3 (1988), 383–4, 386–8.

37. D. Baines, *Emigration from Europe, 1815–1930* (London, 1991), p. 32. Baines, *Migration in a Mature Economy*, pp. 67, 281.

38. C. J. Erickson, 'Emigration from the British Isles to the USA in 1831', *Population Studies*, 35, 2 (1981), 191, 194, 196. C. J. Erickson, 'Emigration from the British Isles to the USA in 1841. Part II. Who Were the English Emigrants?', *Population Studies*, 44, 1 (1990), 22–3, 28, 30, 39. Baines, *Migration in a Mature Economy*, pp. 74–5, 282. W. E. Van Vugt, 'Running from Ruin?' The Emigration of British Farmers to the USA in the Wake of the Repeal of the Corn Laws', *Economic History Review*, XLI, 3 (1988), 415–19, 426. M. Harper, *Emigration from North-East Scotland. Vol. I. Willing Exiles* (Aberdeen, 1988), pp. 344–5.

39. J. D. Gould, 'European Inter-Continental Emigration, 1815–1914: Patterns and Causes', *Journal of European Economic History*, 8, 3 (1979), 611–12, 614. J. D. Gould, 'European Inter-Continental Emigration the Road Home: Return Migration

from the USA', *Journal of European Economic History*, 9, 1 (1980), 51. Baines, *Migration in a Mature Economy*, pp. 127, 132.

40. Baines, *Migration in a Mature Economy*, pp. 166–77, 279–82. Gould, 'European Inter-Continental Emigration, 1815–1914', 614, 618, 650, 659–61. Harper, *Emigration from North-East Scotland*, pp. 343–8. Chesnais, *The Demographic Transition*, p. 159. Massey, 'Economic Development', 396–7. J. D. Gould, 'European Inter-Continental Emigration: The Role of Diffusion and Feedback', *Journal of European Economic History*, 9, 2 (1980), 281, 300. C. J. Erickson, 'Emigration from the British Isles to the USA in 1841. Part I. Emigration from the British Isles', *Population Studies*, 43, 3 (1989), 367.

41. Gould, 'European Inter-Continental Emigration, 1815–1914', 667. Chesnais, *The Demographic Transition*, pp. 154, 160, 165, 168–9, 178–9.

42. W. L. Marr, 'The United Kingdom's International Migration in the Inter-War Period: Theoretical Considerations and Empirical Testing', *Population Studies*, 31, 3 (1977), 574–6, 578. D. Pope, 'Some Factors Inhibiting Australian Immigration in the 1920s', *Australian Economic History Review*, 24, 1 (1984), 34–6, 38–52. Coleman and Salt, *The British Population*, p. 441.

43. For details of this legislation see N. H. Carrier and J. R. Jeffery, *External Migration. A Study of the Available Statistics, 1815–1950* (London, 1953), pp. 35, 37. Marr, 'The United Kingdom's International Migration', 573–4. Gould, 'European Inter-Continental Emigration, 1815–1914', 620. Baines, *Emigration from Europe*, pp. 71–2.

44. Marr, 'The United Kingdom's International Migration', 574.

45. Symptomatic of the economic problems faced by Commonwealth and other New World countries in the 1930s was the withdrawal of the £10 ocean passage rate by the government of Canada and the Australian government's decision to provide assisted passage only to relatives of existing settlers. Carrier and Jeffrey, *External Migration*, p. 37.

46. Coleman and Salt, *The British Population*, pp. 441, 443.

47. D. Friedlander and R. J. Roshier, 'A Study of Internal Migration in England and Wales, Part I', *Population Studies*, 19, 3 (1966), 251–66. Lawton, 'Population Changes in England and Wales in the Later Nineteenth Century', 57, 60, 62, 65. Lawton, 'Regional Population Trends in England and Wales', 32–3, 38. Flinn (ed.), *Scottish Population History*, pp. 461, 463.

S. Nicholas and P. Shergold, 'Internal Migration in England, 1818–39', *Journal of Historical Geography*, 13, 2 (1987), 163–4.

48. Baines, *Migration in a Mature Economy*, pp. 279–80. Nicholas and Shergold, 'Internal Migration', 164–6. Lawton, 'Population Changes in England and Wales in the Later Nineteenth Century', 57, 60, 62. Lawton, 'Regional Population Trends in England and Wales', 38, 40, 46, 66. Friedlander, 'The Spread of Urbanisation', 430. Law, 'The Growth of Urban Population', 132, 135, 138–9.

49. Lawton, 'Regional Population Trends in England and Wales', 32–3, 37–8, 56–7. Coleman and Salt, *The British Population*, p. 410. The interwar period also saw an increase in the average distance of migration. Friedlander and Roshier, 'A Study of Internal Migration', 266–8. Lawton, 'Regional Population Trends in England and Wales', 33–4.

50. Lawton, 'Regional Population Trends in England and Wales', 37–8, 56. Coleman and Salt, *The British Population*, pp. 93–4, 410. Tony Champion, 'Internal Migration and the Spatial Distribution of Population', in Joshi (ed.), *The Changing Population*, p. 121.

51. A. A. Ogilvy, 'Migration – the Influence of Economic Change', *Futures*, October (1979), 383–94. Champion, 'Population Trends in the 1970s', 186, 189, 203. A. A. Ogilvy, 'Population Migration Between the Regions of Great Britain', *Regional Studies*, 16, 1 (1982), 65, 67. Fielding, 'Counterurbanization', 224. Coleman and Salt, *The British Population*, pp. 414–15. I. Balusu, 'Internal Migration in the United Kingdom, 1989', *Population Trends*, 62 (1990), 33. M. Rosenbaum and J. Bailey, 'Movement within England and Wales during the 1980s, As Measured by the N.H.S. Central Register', *Population Trends*, 65 (1991), 25.

52. Coleman and Salt, *The British Population*, pp. 95, 99. Champion, 'Population Trends in the 1970s', 189–90, 201, 203. Stillwell, 'The Analysis and Projections of Interregional Migration', 170. Fielding, 'Counterurbanization', 224. Champion, 'United Kingdom', 83. Ogilvy, 'Population Migration', 62–71. Goddard, 'Structural Change', 15. Champion, 'Internal Migration', 110, 114. Not until the late 1980s did the rest of the South East join Greater London in losing population on net balance of migration. Rosenbaum and Bailey, 'Movement within England and Wales', 26–8.

53. See data in Registrar-General Scotland, *Annual Report 1980*, pp. 281–3 and Registrar-General Scotland, *Annual Report 1990*, p. 109.

54. Balusu, 'Internal Migration', 34–5. Coleman and Salt, *The British Population*, p. 109. Champion, 'Population Trends in the 1970s', 190, 210, 203, 210. Fielding, 'Counterurbanization', 224. Stillwell, 'The Analysis and Projection of Interregional Migration', 178. I. Stillwell, 'Migration between Metropolitan and Non-Metropolitan Regions in the UK', in P. E. White and Bert van der Knaap (eds), *Contemporary Studies of Migration* (Norwich, 1985), p. 22.

55. S. Pollard, *The Development of the British Economy, 1914–90* (London, 1992), pp. 41, 234, 236, 395–6, 398. Coleman and Salt, *The British Population*, pp. 378, 381, 383.

56. For data on regional variations in employment and unemployment levels see Pollard, *The Development of the British Economy*, pp. 279, 404. Coleman and Salt, *The British Population*, pp. 379, 382–4, 387–8, 391. Champion, 'Internal Migration', 115.

57. D. E. Keeble, 'Industrial Decline, Regional Policy and the Urban-Rural Manufacturing Shift in the United Kingdom', *Environment and Planning A*, 12 (1980), 945. Champion, 'Population Trends in the 1970s', 190. Champion, 'United Kingdom', 99–100. Coleman and Salt, *The British Population*, p. 412.

58. Goddard, 'Structural Change', 20.

59. Champion, 'United Kingdom', 90. Champion, 'Internal Migration', 114. Coleman and Salt, *The British Population*, p. 430. Pollard, *The Development of the British Economy*, p. 405.

60. Jones et al., 'Counterurbanization in Societal Context', 437. Jones et al., 'Counterurbanization, 73. Champion, 'Population Trends in the 1970s', 189.

61. C. Hamnett and W. Randolph, 'The Changing Population Distribution of England and Wales, 1961–81: a Clean Break or Consistent Progression?' *Built Environment*, 8, 4 (1982), 272–80. Fielding, 'Counterurbanization', 239–40.

62. Champion, 'United Kingdom', 83. It has been pointed out, however, that the turnaround in net migration between urban and rural areas occurred in rural areas with high as well as low population densities. Fielding, 'Counterurbanization', 241.

63. Champion, 'Recent Changes in the Pace of Population Deconcentration', 398. Coleman and Salt, *The British Population*, pp. 112, 411.

64. Jones et al., 'Counterurbanization in Societal Context', 442, Jones et al., 'Counterurbanization', 73. Fielding, 'Counterurbanization', 240. Champion, 'Recent Changes in the Pace of Population Deconcentration', 397.

65. Mintel, *Regional Life Styles 1992* (London, 1992).

66. A. M. Warnes and C. M. Law, 'The Elderly Population of Great Britain: Locational Trends and Policy Implications', *Transactions of the Institute of British Geographers*, New Series, 9, (1984), 37–59. Champion, 'Recent Changes in the Pace of Population Deconcentration', 397. Champion, 'Counterurbanization', 237, 239–40.

67. Jones et al., 'Peripheral Counterurbanization', 18, 23. See also Jones et al., 'Counterurbanization in Societal Context', 439.

68. A. J. Fielding, 'Counterurbanization in Western Europe', *Progress in Planning*, 17, 1 (1982), 5–34. Fielding, 'Counterurbanization', 240, 242. Goddard, 'Structural Change', 3. Jones et al., 'Counterurbanization in Societal Context', 440–1. Jones et al., 'Counterurbanization', 74–6. Champion, 'Recent Changes in the Pace of Population Deconcentration', 397–8. Champion, 'Conclusion', 235–7, 240. Champion, 'United Kingdom', 98–9. Coleman and Salt, *The British Population*, p. 111.

69. Champion, 'Population Trends in Rural Britain', 22. Champion, 'Recent Changes in the Pace of Population Deconcentration', 347. Jones et al., 'Peripheral Counterurbanization', 16. Jones et al., 'Counterurbanization', 71, 79. Champion, 'United Kingdom', 100.

70. Goddard, 'Structural Change', 7. Coleman and Salt, *The British Population*, p. 98.

71. For details see Keeble, 'Industrial Decline', 945, 948. D. Massey and R. Meegan, *The Anatomy of Job Loss* (London, 1982), p. 189. D. Massey, *Spatial Divisions of Labour* (London, 1984), p. 135. Champion, 'Recent Changes in the Pace of Population Deconcentration', 397. Champion, 'Conclusion', 236. Champion, 'United Kingdom', 96–7. Similar, though less pronounced changes occurred in the location of the service sector. Fielding, 'Counterurbanization', 245.

72. Fielding, 'Counterurbanization', 246. Champion, 'Internal Migration', 121.

73. Fielding, 'Counterurbanization', 244–6. Champion, 'Conclusion', 240.

74. M. F. Dunford, 'The Restructuring of Industrial Space', *International Journal of Urban and Regional Research*, 1 (1977), 510–20. D. E. Keeble, 'Industrial Decline in the Inner City and Conurbation', *Transactions of the Institute of British Geographers*, New Series, 3 (1978), 101–14. Keeble, 'Industrial Decline', 948, 953. S. Fothergill and G. Gudgin, *Unequal Growth. Urban and Regional Employment Change in the U.K.* (London, 1982), pp. 104–12. Fielding, 'Counterurbanization in Western Europe', 31. Fielding,

'Counterurbanization', 246. Goddard, 'Structural Change', 5. D. B. Massey and R. A. Meegan, 'Industrial Restructuring Versus the Cities', *Urban Studies*, 15 (1978), 273–88. D. B. Massey and R. A. Meegan, 'The Geography of Industrial Reorganisation', *Progress in Planning*, 10 (1979), 155–237. Champion, 'Recent Changes in the Pace of Population Deconcentration', 396–7. Champion, 'Conclusion', 240. Champion, 'United Kingdom', 99. Champion, 'Internal Migration', 122. Coleman and Salt, *The British Population*, p. 111.

75. Keeble, 'Industrial Decline', 955, 957. Fielding, 'Counterurbanization in Western Europe', 29–31. Fielding, 'Counterurbanization', 243–4. Goddard, 'Structural Change', 6. Champion, 'Population Trends in the 1970s', 190. Champion, 'Recent Changes in the Pace of Population Deconcentration', 398. Champion, 'United Kingdom', 98–9. Champion, 'Internal Migration', 121–2. Coleman and Salt, *The British Population*, pp. 95, 98, 111–12, 412. D. E. C. Eversley, 'Population Changes and Regional Policies since the War', *Regional Studies*, 5 (1971), 211–17.

76. Keeble, 'Industrial Decline in the Inner City', 101–14. Massey and Meegan, 'Industrial Restructuring', 273–88. Champion, 'Recent Changes in the Pace of Population Deconcentration', 391, 397–8. Champion, 'United Kingdom', 99–100. Champion, 'Internal Migration', 124. Champion, 'Population Trends in the 1970s', 213. Coleman and Salt, *The British Population*, p. 414.

77. Goddard, 'Structural Change', 14. Champion, 'Recent Changes in the Pace of Population Deconcentration', 398. Champion, 'Population Trends in the 1970s', 192, 194, 213–14. Champion, 'Internal Migration', 124.

78. Champion, 'Population Trends in Rural Britain', 22. Champion, 'Population Trends in the 1970s', 191–4, 213–14. Champion, 'Recent Changes in the Pace of Population Deconcentration', 397. Champion, 'United Kingdom', 100. Champion, 'Internal Migration', 123–4. Goddard, 'Structural Change', 14, 19–20. Coleman and Salt, *The British Population*, p. 414. Champion, 'Conclusion', 240.

3 MORTALITY

1. See also D. Friedlander, J. Schellekens, E. Ben-Mosche and A. Keysar, 'Socio-Economic Characteristics and Life Expectancies in Nineteenth Century England: a District Analysis', *Population*

Studies, 39, 1 (1985), 138, 140. T. B. Gage, 'The Decline of Mortality in England and Wales 1861 to 1964: Decomposition By Cause of Death and Component of Mortality', *Population Studies*, 47, 1 (1993), 53.

2. Chesnais, *The Demographic Transition*, pp. 54–5.

3. R. I. Armitage, 'English Regional Fertility and Mortality Patterns, 1975–85', *Population Trends*, 47 (1987), 19.

4. B. Benjamin, 'Variations of Mortality in the United Kingdom with Special Reference to Immigrants and Minority Groups', in Coleman (ed.), *Demography of Immigrants*, p. 46.

5. Average life expectancy at birth in England between 1551–75 and 1776–1800 varied from a low of 33 to a high of 39 years and then rose from 39 for the cohort born between 1801 and 1825 to 40 (1826–50), 41 (1851–75) and 46 (1876–1900). R. Woods, *The Population of Britain in the Nineteenth Century* (London, 1992), p. 29.

6. S. H. Preston, 'The Changing Relation Between Mortality and Level of Economic Development', *Population Studies*, 29, 2 (1975), 244.

7. Compared with other countries, the age pattern of early British mortality decline was unusual. S. H. Preston and V. E. Nelson, 'Structure and Change in Causes of Death: an International Summary', *Population Studies*, 28, 1 (1974), 19–51.

8. T. McKeown and R. G. Record, 'Reasons for the Decline of Mortality in England and Wales during the Nineteenth Century', *Population Studies*, 16, 2 (1962), 100–1. R. I. Woods, P. A. Watterson and J. H. Woodward, 'The Causes of Rapid Infant Mortality Decline in England and Wales, 1861–1921. Part I', *Population Studies*, 42, 3 (1988), 348–9. J. M. Winter, 'The Decline of Mortality in Britain, 1870–1950', in Barker and Drake (eds), *Population and Society*, pp. 103–4. Woods, *The Population of Britain*, p. 57. Gage, 'The Decline of Mortality', 53–4, 64.

9. C. H. Lee, 'Regional Inequalities in Infant Mortality in Britain, 1861–1971: Patterns and Hypotheses', *Population Studies*, 45, 1 (1991), 58–9, 61.

10. Woods et al., 'The Causes of Rapid Infant Mortality Decline I', 348.

11. J. M. Winter, 'Some Aspects of the Demographic Consequences of the First World War in Britain', *Population Studies*, 30, 3 (1976), 547–8. J. M. Winter, 'The Impact of the First World War on Civilian Health in Britain', *Economic History Review*, 30, 3 (1977), 489, 493–4. J. M. Winter, 'Infant Mortality, Maternal Mortality and Public Health in Britain in the 1930s', *Journal of*

European Economic History, 13, 2 (1979), 443. J. M. Winter, 'Aspects of the Impact of the First World War on Infant Mortality in Britain', *Journal of European Economic History*, 11, 3 (1972), 714, 716, 720. For the 1980s see OPCS, 'A Review of the 1980s', *Population Trends*, 62 (1990), 14. See also J. Hellier, 'Perinatal Mortality, 1950–73', *Population Trends*, 10 (1977), 13–15. J. F. Forbes, F. A. Boddy, R. Pickering and M. M. Wyllie, 'Perinatal Mortality in Scotland, 1970–9', *Journal of Epidemiology and Community Health*, 36 (1982), 282–8.

12. CSO, *Annual Abstract of Statistics 1993* (London, 1993), p. 39. Winter, 'Infant Mortality', 454. Winter 'The Decline of Mortality', 104. I. Loudon, 'Maternal Mortality: 1880–1950. Some Regional and International Comparisons', *Society for the Social History of Medicine*, 1 (1988), 183, 187, 189–90, 196. I. Loudon, 'On Maternal and Infant Mortality, 1900–60', *Society for the Social History of Medicine*, 4 (1991), 37–40. E. Fox, 'Powers of Life and Death: Aspects of Maternal Welfare in England and Wales between the Wars', *Medical History*, 35 (1991), 332.

13. A. R. Thatcher, 'Trends in Numbers and Mortality at High Ages in England and Wales', *Population Studies*, 46, 3 (1992), 419–20.

14. In part due to an increase in the percentage of the age group aged 40–4. Both in Scotland and England/Wales, however, mortality among males aged 15–24 and 25–34 was also higher in 1990 than in 1985. In Scotland death rates among females aged 25–34 and 35–44 fell between 1985 and 1990 but those among females aged 15–24 did not. In England and Wales the mortality rates of females aged 25–34 rose in the second half of the 1980s while those of females aged 15–24 and 35–44 remained unchanged. K. Dunnell, 'Deaths among 15–44 year olds', *Population Trends*, 64 (1991), 38–43.

15. Winter, 'Some Aspects', 545.

16. Lee, 'Regional Inequalities', 57, 60–1. Winter, 'The Impact of the First World War', 495. Winter, 'Infant Mortality', 446–7. Benjamin, 'Variations of Mortality', 49. Coleman and Salt, *The British Population*, p. 320. B. Botting and A. J. Macfarlane, 'Geographic Variation in Infant Mortality in Relation to Birthweight, 1983–85', in M. Britton, *Mortality and Geography. A Review in the Mid 1980s England and Wales, Series DS No. 9*, (London, 1990), pp. 647–51.

17. Woods, The Population of Britain, p. 58. Friedlander et al., 'Socio-Economic Characteristics', 139–40. R. Woods, 'The Effects of Population Redistribution on the Level of Mortality

in Nineteenth Century England and Wales', *Journal of Economic History*, 45, 3 (1985), 647–51.

18. Winter, 'The Decline of Mortality', 101, 103.
19. P. H. Curson, 'Mortality Patterns in the Modern World', in Pacione (ed.), *Population Geography*, p. 115. F. W. A. Van Poppel, 'Regional Mortality Differences in Western Europe: a Review of the Situation in the Seventies', *Social Science and Medicine*, 15D, 3 (1981), 341–52. P. L. Knox, 'Convergence and Divergence in Regional Patterns of Infant Mortality in the United Kingdom from 1949–51 to 1970–1', *Social Science and Medicine*, 15D, 3 (1981), 323–8. A. M. Adelstein and J. S. A. Ashley, 'Recent Trends in Mortality and Morbidity in England and Wales', in R. W. Hiorns (ed.), *Demographic Patterns in Developed Societies* (London, 1980), pp. 150–1. Armitage, 'English Regional Fertility', 1923. Coleman and Salt, *The British Population*, p. 320.
20. Friedlander et al., 'Socio-Economic Characteristics', 139. Social class differentials in infant mortality on the other hand widened between 1895–7 and 1910. Woods, *The Population of Britain*, pp. 58–9.
21. Woods, *The Population of Britain*, pp. 58–9. Winter, 'Infant Mortality', 451. Winter, 'The Decline of Mortality', 108. Benjamin, 'Variations of Mortality', 52–3. Curson, 'Mortality Patterns', 100–4.
22. Curson, 'Mortality Patterns', 98–9, 101. Benjamin, 'Variations of Mortality', 52. Coleman and Salt, *The British Population*, pp. 314–15, 318–19. E. R. Pamuk, 'Social Class Inequality in Mortality from 1921 to 1972 in England and Wales', *Population Studies*, 39, 1 (1985), 19, 27. Standardised Mortality Ratios allow for the effect on death rates of variations in a population's age structure.
23. Winter, 'The Decline of Mortality', 108–9. For further details see McKeown and Record, 'Reasons for the Decline of Mortality'. T. McKeown, *The Modern Rise of Population* (London, 1976). Preston and Nelson, 'Structure and Change'. S. H. Preston, *Mortality Patterns in National Population with Special Reference to Recorded Causes of Death* (London, 1976). T. McKeown, *The Origins of Human Disease* (Oxford, 1988). H. C. Trowell and D. P. Burkitt, *Western Diseases: Their Emergence and Prevention* (London, 1981). F. B. Smith, *The Retreat of Tuberculosis, 1850–1950* (London, 1988). W. P. D. Logan, 'Mortality in England and Wales from 1848–1947', *Population Studies*, 4, 2 (1980). Gage, 'The Decline of Mortality'. Benjamin,

'Variations of Mortality', 48–9. Coleman and Salt, *The British Population*, pp. 238, 274.

24. Curson, 'Mortality Patterns', 116, 118.

25. T. McKeown, R. G. Brown and R. G. Record, 'An Interpretation of the Modern Rise of Population in Europe', *Population Studies*, 26, 3 (1972), 349. T. McKeown, R. G. Record and R. D. Turner, 'An Interpretation of the Decline in Mortality in England and Wales During the 20th Century', *Population Studies*, 29, 3 (1975), 391, 421.

26. Lee, 'Regional Inequalities', 59. Woods et al., 'The Causes of Rapid Infant Mortality Decline I', 362.

27. Coleman and Salt, *The British Population*, p. 54. A. J. Mercer, *Disease, Mortality and Population in Transition. Epidemiology-Demographic Change in England Since the Eighteenth Century as Part of a Global Phenomenon* (Leicester, 1990), pp. 122, 167. Loudon, 'Maternal Mortality', 199–200.

28. McKeown and Record, 'Reasons for the Decline of Mortality', 120. McKeown et al., 'An Interpretation of the Modern Rise of Population', 357. McKeown et al., 'An Interpretation of the Decline in Mortality', 421–2.

29. Winter, 'Some Aspects', 547–8. Winter, 'The Impact of the First World War', 499–501. Winter, 'Infant Mortality', 462. Winter, 'The Decline of Mortality', 112, 114–16. Winter, 'Aspects', 727–8.

30. B. Supple, 'Income and Demand, 1860–1914', in R. Floud and D. McCloskey (eds), *The Economic History of Britain since 1700. vol. 2. 1860 to the 1970s* (Cambridge, 1981), p. 135. P. Thane, 'Social History, 1860–1914', in Floud and McCloskey (eds), *The Economic History of Britain*, p. 202.

31. D. J. Oddy, 'The Health of the People', in Barker and Drake (eds), *Population and Society*, p. 125.

32. Mercer, *Disease*, pp. 120–1, 169. A. J. Mercer, 'Relative Trends in Mortality from Related Respiratory and Airborne Infectious Diseases', *Population Studies*, 40, 1 (1986), 130, 132, 145. R. I. Woods and P. R. A. Hinde, 'Mortality in Victorian England: Models and Patterns', *Journal of Interdisciplinary History*, 18 (1987), 53.

33. Mercer, 'Relative Trends', 132.

34. Loudon, 'Maternal Mortality', 186, 196–8, 208, 222. Fox, 'Powers of Life', 333–4.

35. Preston, 'The Changing Relation', 237–8, 240, 244.

36. P. A. Watterson, 'Role of the Environment in the Decline of Infant Mortality: an Analysis of the 1911 Census of England and Wales', *Journal of Biosocial Science*, 18 (1986), 457, 468. P. A.

Watterson, 'Infant Mortality Decline by Father's Occupation from the 1911 Census of England and Wales', *Demography*, 25, 2 (1988), 300–3.

37. M. H. Brenner, 'Mortality and the National Economy: a Review of the Experience of England and Wales, 1936–76', *The Lancet* (1979), 568–73. J. Stern, 'The Relationship between Unemployment, Morbidity and Mortality in Britain', *Population Studies*, 37, 1 (1983), 73, I. D. McAvinchey, 'Economic Factors and Mortality. Some Aspects of the Scottish Case, 1950–78', *Scottish Journal of Political Economy*, 31, 1 (1984), 17.

38. Benjamin, 'Variations of Mortality', 48–9. Pamuk, 'Social Class', 28. Coleman and Salt, *The British Population*, pp. 258–9, 280–8, 295, 345, 350, 352–3, 355. R. T. Ravenholt, 'Tobacco's Global Death March', *Population and Development Review*, 16 (1990), 213–40.

39. Loudon, 'Maternal Mortality', 195, 197–9. Fox, 'Powers of Life', 331, 333, 335. Winter, 'Infant Mortality', 455–60.

40. Hellier, 'Perinatal Mortality', 13–15. Forbes et al, 'Perinatal Mortality', 282–8. Coleman and Salt, *The British Population*, p. 335.

41. Coleman and Salt, *The British Population*, pp. 54, 274, 279. Stern, 'The Relationship', 74. For evidence on the importance of variations in medical provision for regional and class differences in mortality see Coleman and Salt, *The British Population*, pp. 356–7, 363. Loudon, 'Maternal Mortality', 222. Curson, 'Mortality Patterns', 98–100. Pamuk, 'Social Class', 28–9. Brenner, 'Variations of Mortality', 52.

42. McKeown et al., 'An Interpretation of the Decline in Mortality', 421–2.

43. Friedlander et al., 'Socio-Economic Characteristics', 137–8.

44. R. I. Woods, P. A. Watterson and J. H. Woodward, 'The Causes of Rapid Infant Mortality Decline in England and Wales', 1861–1921. Part II', *Population Studies*, 43, 1 (1989), 129–32. Winter, 'Some Aspects', 548. Winter, 'The Impact of the First World War', 496–8. Winter, 'Aspects', 724–7. Woods, *The Population of Britain*, pp. 65, 67. M. W. Beaver, 'Population, Infant Mortality and Milk', *Population Studies*, 27, 2 (1973), 243. C. Dyhouse, 'Working Class Mothers and Infant Mortality in England, 1895–1914', *Journal of Social History*, 12, 2 (1978), 248, 250, 262. Loudon, 'Maternal Mortality', 185–6, 192. Fox, 'Powers of Life', 329, 339. Winter, 'The Decline of Mortality', 109. Coleman and Salt, *The British Population*, pp. 45–6, 53, 278–9.

45. Winter, 'The Decline of Mortality', 110–11. Preston, 'The Changing Relation', 240, 243–4. Mercer, *Disease*, pp. 168–9. Chesnais, *The Demographic Transition*, pp. 54–5, 76, 83.
46. Friedlander, 'Socio-Economic Characteristics', 141–2, 144, 146–7, 151. See also Woods, 'The Effects of Population Redistribution', 647–51. Increasing regional inequalities in infant mortality in Scotland between 1871 and 1921 were largely the result of the rapid growth of mining and heavy industry in particular regions. The relative importance of mining and heavy industry in the economy together with relatively high housing densities also help to explain why infant death rates in Scotland between 1912 and the 1970s were higher than in England and Wales. Lee, 'Regional Inequalities', 61, 63–4.
47. Winter, 'The Decline of Mortality', 109–17.
48. McKeown et al., 'An Interpretation of the Decline of Mortality', 422.
49. Mercer, *Disease*, pp. 94–5, 121–3. Friedlander et al., 'Socio-Economic Characteristics', 138, 151. Beaver, 'Population', 252–3. Watterson, 'Role of the Environment', 457–8, 468. Watterson, 'Infant Mortality Decline', 289, 300–2. Coleman and Salt, *The British Population*, pp. 53, 55, 57–60, 242, 289, 293. Winter, 'The Impact of the First World War', 501. For criticisms of the contribution of pasteurisation and new 'artificial' infant foods to the decline in infant mortality see Dyhouse, 'Working Class Mothers', 255–7.
50. Mercer, *Disease*, p. 168.
51. Preston, 'Changing Relation', 240, 243–4. Coleman and Salt, *The British Population*, pp. 57, 297. Chesnais, *The Demographic Transition*, pp. 78, 83. J. C. Caldwell, 'Education as a Factor in Mortality Decline: an Examination of Nigerian Data', *Population Studies*, 33, 3 (1979), 391, 395–6, 409–13.

4   FERTILITY

1. Woods, *The Population of Britain*, p. 29. C. Wilson and R. I. Woods, 'Fertility in England: a Long-Term Perspective', *Population Studies*, 45, 3 (1991), 403.
2. D. V. Glass, 'Fertility Trends in Europe since the Second World War', *Population Studies*, 22, 1 (1968), 103.
3. M. S. Teitelbaum, *The British Fertility Decline* (Princeton, NJ, 1984), pp. 86–9.

4. W. Brass and M. Kabir, 'Regional Variations in Fertility and Child Mortality during the Demographic Transition in England and Wales', in Hobcraft and Rees (eds), *Regional Demographic Development*, pp. 73–4. At the smaller unit of the registration district there was more variation in the pace of fertility decline. R. I. Woods and C. W. Smith, 'The Decline of Marital Fertility in the Late 19th Century: the Case of England and Wales', *Population Studies*, 37, 2 (1983), 215.

5. Coleman and Salt, *The British Population*, p. 115.

6. G. Calot and C. Blayo, 'Recent Course of Fertility in Western Europe', *Population Studies*, 36, 3 (1982), 350–1.

7. Coleman and Salt, *The British Population*, p. 117.

8. J. Simons, 'Developments in the Interpretation of Recent Fertility Trends in England and Wales', in Hobcraft and Rees (eds), *Regional Demographic Development*, pp. 117–18. M. Murphy, 'Economic Models of Fertility in Post-War Britain – a Conceptual and Statistical Reinterpretation', *Population Studies*, 46, 2 (1992), 235. J. Bourgeois-Pichat, 'The Unprecedented Shortage of Births in Europe', in K. Davis, M. S. Bernstam and R. Ricardo-Campbell (eds), 'Below-Replacement. Fertility in Industrial Societies. Causes, Consequences, Policies', *Population and Development Review*, Supplement to vol. 12 (1986), 10. S. H. Preston, 'The Decline of Fertility in Non-European Industrialized Countries', in Davis et al. (eds), 'Below-Replacement', 26. Calot and Blayo, 'Recent Course of Fertility', 349.

9. E. Overton, 'The Decline in Fertility since 1964: The United Kingdom by Population Groups', in D. Eversley and W. Kolmann (eds), *Population Changes and Social Planning* (London, 1982), p. 34.

10. B. Werner, 'Fertility Trends in Different Social Classes, 1970–83', *Population Trends*, 41 (1985), 8.

11. Recent estimates of fertility by Brass suggest that crude birth rate data somewhat overstate the trend from baby boom to baby bust. W. Brass, 'Is Britain Facing the Twilight of Parenthood?', in Joshi (ed.), *The Changing Population*, pp. 24–5. Total Period Fertility rates, a more satisfactory measure of fertility than crude birth rates because they are free from the effect of changes in age structure, confirm the modest nature of the recovery in fertility in the late 1970s. See data in Armitage, 'English Regional Fertility and Mortality Patterns', 16, 23. J. Craig, 'Fertility Trends within the United Kingdom', *Population Trends*, 67 (1992), 17. J. Craig, 'Recent Fertility Trends in Europe',

Population Trends, 68 (1992), 20. OPCS, 'A Review of the 1980s', *Population Trends*, 62 (1990), 6, 8–9.

12. Coleman and Salt, *The British Population*, pp. 118–9. Calot and Blayo, 'Recent Course of Fertility', 349–51, 353, 372. Bourgeois-Pichat, 'The Unprecedented Shortage', 3, 5, 13. Murphy, 'Economic Models', 235. Craig, 'Recent Fertility Trends', 20. S. Kendrick, F. Bechhofer and D. McCrone, 'Recent Trends in Fertility Differentials in Scotland', in Jones (ed.), *Population Change in Contemporary Scotland*, p. 35.

13. Simons, 'Developments', 122. Craig, 'Fertility Trends', 19. Calot and Blayo, 'Recent Course of Fertility', 353, 372. Kendrick et al., 'Recent Trends', 37. Armitage, 'English Regional Fertility and Mortality Patterns', 17, 23. J. Coward, 'Fertility Patterns in the Modern World', in Pacione (ed.), *Population Geography*, pp. 70, 75, 81.

14. Craig, 'Recent Fertility Trends', 17–19. Kendrick et al., 'Recent Trends', 35. Overton, 'The Decline in Fertility', 46.

15. Coleman and Salt, *The British Population*, p. 167. Werner, 'Fertility Trends', 11–12. For the socio-occupational structure of illegitimacy in earlier times see N. Rogers, 'Carnal Knowledge: Illegitimacy in Eighteenth Century Westminster', *Journal of Social History*, 23 (1989), 358. N. L. Tranter, 'Illegitimacy in Nineteenth Century Rural Scotland: a Puzzle Resolved?', *International Journal of Sociology and Social Policy*, 5, 2 (1985), 41. The percentage of children conceived before marriage also varied inversely with socio-occupational class. J. Haskey, 'Social Class and Socio-Economic Differentials in Divorce in England and Wales', *Population Studies*, 38, 3 (1984), 434.

16. P. Laslett and K. Oosterveen, 'Long-Term Trends in Bastardy in England: a Study of Illegitimacy Figures in the Parish Registers and in the Reports of the Registrar-General, 1561–1960', *Population Studies*, 27, 2 (1973), 276–7. Teitelbaum, *The British Fertility Decline*, pp. 147–9.

17. Craig, 'Fertility Trends', 20.

18. Teitelbaum, *The British Fertility Decline*, p. 149. T. Smout, 'Aspects of Sexual Behaviour in Nineteenth Century Scotland', in A. A. MacLaren (ed.), *Social Class in Scotland* (Edinburgh, 1976), p. 63. I. Carter, 'Illegitimate Births and Illegitimate Inferences', *Scottish Journal of Sociology*, 1 (1976), 125. Coward, 'Fertility Patterns', 84.

19. Coleman and Salt, *The British Population*, p. 135. Laslett and Oosterveen, 'Long-Term Trends', 260–3. B. Werner, 'Recent Trends in Illegitimate Births and Extra-Marital Conceptions',

Population Trends, 30 (1982), 9–10. Werner, 'Fertility Trends', 12. K. Kiernan, 'The Family: Formation and Fission', in Joshi (ed.), *The Changing Population*, pp. 27, 36–7. J. Cooper, 'Births Outside Marriage: Recent Trends and Associated Demographic and Social Changes', *Population Trends*, 63 (1991), 9–10. C. Jones, 'Fertility of the Over Thirties', *Population Trends*, 67 (1992), 13. Craig, 'Fertility Trends', 20. B. Werner, 'Trends in First, Second and Later Births', *Population Trends*, 45 (1986), 29–30.

20. E. Shorter, J. Knodel and E. Van de Walle, 'The Decline of Non-Marital Fertility in Europe, 1880–1940', *Population Studies*, 25, 3 (1971), 375.

21. Bourgeois-Pichat, 'The Unprecedented Shortage', 13, 15. Similar increases in illegitimacy occurred in Australia, Canada, New Zealand and the USA from the early 1960s. In Japan, by contrast, levels of bastardy declined. Preston, 'The Decline of Fertility', 35–6.

22. From data in Bourgeois-Pichat, 'The Unprecedented Shortage', 15. Cooper, 'Births Outside Marriage', 8. Kiernan, 'The Family', 40. Werner, 'Recent Trends', 9. Levels of bastardy were similar in Australia, Canada, New Zealand and the USA. Preston, 'The Decline of Fertility', 36. In the USA in 1989, for example, 27 per cent of all births were illegitimate. US Bureau of the Census, *Statistical Abstract of the United States 1992* (Washington, 1992), p. 69.

23. Laslett and Oosterveen, 'Long-Term Trends', 256. Shorter et al., 'The Decline of Non-Marital Fertility', 380. P. Laslett, *Family Life and Illicit Love in Earlier Generations* (Cambridge, 1977), pp. 105–6.

24. Laslett and Oosterveen, 'Long-Term Trends', 256, 286. Laslett, *Family Life*, p. 107.

25. L. A. Tilly, J. W. Scott and M. Cohen, 'Women's Work and European Fertility Patterns', *Journal of Interdisciplinary History*, VI, 3 (1976), 475.

26. N. F. R. Crafts, 'Illegitimacy in England and Wales in 1911', *Population Studies*, 36, 2 (1982), 329–31. J. Coward, 'The Analysis of Regional Fertility Patterns', in Woods and Rees (eds), *Population Structure*, p. 64.

27. Shorter et al., 'The Decline of Non-Marital Fertility', 382, 392–3. E. Shorter, 'Female Emancipation, Birth Control and Fertility in European History', *American Historical Review*, 78, 3 (1973), 612–33. E. Shorter, *The Making of the Modern Family* (London, 1977), pp. 86–124. M. S. Hindus, 'Pre-Marital Pregnancy in America 1640–1971: an Overview and

Interpretation', *Journal of Interdisciplinary History*, V, 4 (1975), 537–70. Kiernan, 'The Family', 30–1.

28. Laslett and Oosterveen, 'Long-Term Trends', 256.
29. See p. 97.
30. On trends in divorce and extra-marital conception see pp. 92, 96. Rates of premarital conception in England and Wales roughly halved between the late nineteenth and mid twentieth century, rose from around 13 per cent in 1955 to 22 per cent in 1967 and fell to around 16 per cent after the mid 1970s. See data in Coleman and Salt, *The British Population*, p. 154. D. J. Van de Kaa, 'Recent Trends in Fertility in Western Europe', in Hiorns (ed.), *Demographic Patterns*, p. 64. Werner, 'Recent Trends', 12. Simons, 'Developments', 121–2. Kiernan, 'The Family', 31.
31. Kiernan, 'The Family', 30–1.
32. Coleman and Salt, *The British Population*, pp. 136, 154.
33. See pp. 100, 112, 125.
34. Bourgeois-Pichat, 'The Unprecedented Shortage', 3, 14. Preston, 'The Decline of Fertility', 35. Cooper, 'Births Outside Marriage', 8–10, 12, 14–15, 17.
35. Wilson and Woods, 'Fertility in England', 399, 406–7. M. R. Haines, 'Fertility, Nuptiality and Occupation: a Study of British Mid-Nineteenth Century Coalmining Populations', *Journal of Interdisciplinary History*, VIII, 2 (1977), 278–80. Woods, *The Population of Britain*, pp. 48–9.
36. Coleman and Salt, *The British Population*, p. 62. Teitelbaum, *The British Fertility Decline*, p. 106.
37. Coleman and Salt, *The British Population*, p. 134.
38. D. A. Coleman, 'Recent Trends in Marriage and Divorce in Britain and Europe', in Hiorns (ed.), *Demographic Patterns*, p. 122. S. C. Watkins, 'Regional Patterns of Nuptiality in Europe 1870–1960', *Population Studies*, 35, 2 (1981), 214–15. Glass, 'Fertility Trends', 105, 107. Preston, 'The Decline of Fertility', 30. Coleman and Salt, *The British Population*, pp. 180, 182. J. Hajnal, 'Age at Marriage and Proportions Marrying', *Population Studies*, 7, 2 (1953), 111–23.
39. Coleman and Salt, *The British Population*, pp. 182, 185. Coleman, 'Recent Trends', 88.
40. Glass, 'Fertility Trends', 105, 110. Coleman and Salt, *The British Population*, p. 135. Simons, 'Developments', 123. Overton, 'The Decline in Fertility', 37. J. Busfield and G. Hawthorn, 'Some Social Determinants of Recent Trends in British Fertility', *Journal of Biosocial Science*, Sup. 3 (1977), 66. M. Ni Bhrolchain,

'Period Parity Progression Ratios and Birth Intervals in England and Wales 1941–71: a Synthetic Life Table Analysis', *Population Studies*, 41, 1 (1987), 120. S. M. Farid, 'The Current Tempo of Fertility in England and Wales', *Population Studies*, 28, 1 (1974), 83. J. F. Ermisch, 'The Relevance of the Easterlin Hypothesis and the "New Home Economics" to Fertility Movement in Great Britain', *Population Studies*, 33, 1 (1979), 48.

41. Summary of nuptiality trends based on data and discussion in Coleman, 'Recent Trends', 88, 122. R. Leete, 'Marriage and Divorce', *Population Trends*, 3 (1976), 3–8. Kiernan, 'The Family', 27–8, 33. Busfield and Hawthorn, 'Some Social Determinants', 66–7. S. Eldridge and K. Kiernan, 'Declining First Marriage Rates in England and Wales: a Change in Timing or a Rejection of Marriage?', *European Journal of Population*, 1 (1985), 327–8, 335, 344. S. M. Farid, 'Cohort Nuptiality in England and Wales', *Population Studies*, 30, 1 (1976), 150–1. J. F. Ermisch, 'Economic Opportunities, Marriage Squeezes and the Propensity to Marry: an Economic Analysis of Period Marriage Rates in England and Wales', *Population Studies*, 35, 3 (1981), 347. J. Haskey, 'Marital Status before Marriage and Age at Marriage: Their Influence on the Chance of Divorce', *Population Trends*, 64 (1991), 4, 6. Glass, 'Fertility Trends', 130. R. Schoen and J. Baj, 'Twentieth Century Cohort Marriage and Divorce in England and Wales', *Population Studies*, 38, 3 (1984), 447–8. C. F. Westhoff, 'Perspective on Nuptiality and Fertility', in Davis et al. (eds), Below-Replacement, 155. J. M. Winter, 'War, Family and Fertility in Twentieth Century Europe', in J. R. Gillis, L. A. Tilly and D. Levine (eds), *The European Experience of Declining Fertility. A Quiet Revolution, 1850–1970* (Oxford, 1992), pp. 300–2. Throughout the twentieth century ages at marriage have correlated positively with social class. Coleman and Salt, *The British Population*, p. 190.

42. Teitelbaum, *The British Fertility Decline*, pp. 97–103. M. Anderson and D. J. Morse, 'High Fertility, High Emigration, Low Nuptiality: Adjustment Processes in Scotland's Demographic Experience, 1861–1914, Part II', *Population Studies*, 47, 2 (1993), 319. Watkins, 'Regional Patterns', 215. S. C. Watkins, 'From Local to National Communities: the Transformation of Demographic Regimes in Western Europe, 1870–1960', *Population and Development Review*, 16, 2 (1990), 242, 247.

43. Figures from Kiernan, 'The Family'. 34, J. Ermisch, 'Divorce: Economic Antecedents and Aftermath', in Joshi (ed.), *The Changing Population*, p. 42. CSO, *Annual Abstract of Statistics 1993* (London, 1993), p. 24. See also Coleman, 'Recent Trends',

93–4. Coleman and Salt, *The British Population*, pp. 192–3, 196, 199. Schoen and Baj, 'Twentieth Century Cohort Marriage', 439, 448. Haskey, 'Marital Status', 4, 11. Haskey, 'Social Class', 419. J. Haskey, 'Social Class Differentials in Remarriage after Divorce: Results of a Forward Linkage Study', *Population Trends*, 47 (1987), 34. Preston, 'The Decline of Fertility', 33–4. Bourgeois-Pichat, 'The Unprecedented Shortage', 3. R. Lesthaeghe, 'A Century of Demographic and Cultural Change in Western Europe: an Explanation of Underlying Dimensions', *Population and Development Review*, 9, 3 (1983), 416.

44. Haskey, 'Social Class', 424–5, 430, 436–7. Coleman and Salt, *The British Population*, pp. 200–1.

45. Coleman and Salt, *The British Population*, pp. 203, 205.

46. Haskey, 'Social Class Differentials', 34. Except in West Germany the decline was more pronounced in western Europe. Lesthaeghe, 'A Century', 416–17.

47. A. Brown and K. Kiernan, 'Cohabitation in Great Britain: Evidence from the General Household Survey', *Population Trends*, 25 (1981), 4–10. Eldridge and Kiernan, 'Declining First Marriage Rates', 329. Cooper, 'Births Outside Marriage', 10. Kiernan, 'The Family', 27, 31. In spite of the increase the extent of cohabitation in Britain at the end of the 1980s was less than in a number of other western and northern European countries. Eldridge and Kiernan, 'Declining First Marriage Rates', 344. Kiernan, 'The Family', 32.

48. Van de Kaa, 'Recent Trends', 111–12. D. Gittins, 'Married Life and Birth Control Between the Wars', *Oral History*, III, 2 (1975), 57, 62. Winter, 'War, Family and Fertility', 292, 299. J. M. Winter, 'Britain's "Lost Generation" of the First World War', *Population Studies*, 31, 3 (1977), 452, 465. D. Friedlander, 'The British Depression and Nuptiality: 1873–1896', *Journal of Interdisciplinary History*, XXIII, 1 (1992), 29.

49. Anderson and Morse, 'High Fertility', 340–1.

50. Coward, 'The Analysis of Regional Fertility Patterns', 64.

51. Watkins, 'Regional Patterns', 206–11, 214. Watkins, 'From Local to National', 244–5, 251–2, 254–5, 257–9. S. C. Watkins, 'Demographic Nationalism in Western Europe, 1870–1960', in Gillis et al. (eds), *The European Experience*, pp. 270–90.

52. Glass, 'Fertility Trends', 105. Busfield and Hawthorn, 'Some Social Determinants', 70–1. Van de Kaa, 'Recent Trends', 115. Coleman and Salt, *The British Population*, p. 143. Ermisch, 'Economic Opportunities', 355. J. Ermisch, 'Investigations into the Causes of the Postwar Fertility Swings', in Eversley and

Kolmann (eds), *Population Change*, p. 153. Simons, 'Developments', 123–4. Winter, 'War, Family and Fertility', 306–8.

53. Van de Kaa, 'Recent Trends', 115. Coleman and Salt, *The British Population*, p. 138. Brass, 'Is Britain Facing the Twilight of Parenthood?', 16.

54. Ermisch, 'Investigations', 150. R. Lesthaeghe and D. Meekers, 'Value Changes and the Dimensions of Familism in the European Community', *European Journal of Population*, 2 (1986), 228, 262.

55. Ermisch, 'Economic Opportunities', 347–9, 352, 354–5. Ermisch, 'Investigations', 149–51, 155. J. F. Ermisch, 'The Labour Market in Historical Development', in Eversley and Kolmann (eds), *Population Change*, pp. 158–9, 171, 175, 177. Westhoff, 'Perspective', 159.

56. Ermisch, 'Economic Opportunities', 350–6. Ermisch, 'Investigations', 151. Lesthaeghe, 'A Century', 418–19, 430–1. Westhoff, 'Perspective', 155–7, 159. Preston, 'The Decline of Fertility', 33. Winter, 'War, Family and Fertility', 303. Bourgeois-Pichat, 'The Unprecedented Shortage', 3. Kiernan, 'The Family', 31–2.

57. For examples of the influences of nuptiality see Wilson and Woods, 'Fertility in England', 411, 414. D. Friedlander, 'Demographic Patterns and Socio-Economic Characteristics of the Coalmining Population in England and Wales during the Nineteenth Century', *Economic Development and Cultural Change*, 22 (1973), 39–51. Coward, 'Fertility Patterns', 77–80. Overton, 'The Decline in Fertility', 37–8. R. Lesthaeghe and J. Surkyn, 'Cultural Dynamics and Economic Theories of Fertility Change', *Population and Development Review*, 14 (1988), 30.

58. Brass and Kabir, 'Regional Variations', 73–4.

59. Summary of postwar marital fertility trends based on data and discussion in Farid, 'The Current Tempo', 82–3. Simons, 'Developments', 121–2. Overton, 'The Decline in Fertility', 39, 45. Werner, 'Trends', 28. B. Werner, 'Birth Intervals: Results from the OPCS Longitudinal Study 1972–84', *Population Trends*, 51 (1988), 29. Ni Bhrolchain, 'Period Parity', 120–1, 123. Armitage, 'English Regional Fertility and Mortality Patterns', 16. Coleman and Salt, *The British Population*, pp. 148, 151–2. Craig, 'Fertility Trends', 18. Craig, 'Recent Fertility Trends', 22–3. Jones, 'Fertility of the Over Thirties', 10–11, 14, 16. Glass, 'Fertility Trends', 110, 116, 118. Calot and Blayo, 'Recent Course of Fertility', 356.

60. Wilson and Woods, 'Fertility in England', 414. Teitelbaum, *The British Fertility Decline*, pp. 127–43. Coward, 'The Analysis of Regional Fertility Patterns', 58. Kendrick et al., 'Recent Trends', 33. Watkins, 'From Local to National', 242, 244, 246–7.

61. Woods and Smith, 'The Decline of Marital Fertility', 223–4. Glass, 'Fertility Trends', 118. Overton, 'The Decline in Fertility', 48. Watkins, 'From Local to National', 250. Murphy, 'Economic Models', 243. Coleman and Salt, *The British Population*, pp. 161–2. Haines, 'Fertility', 253. Kendrick et al., 'Recent Trends', 41, 43. Coward, 'Fertility Patterns', 71, 73–4. Werner, 'Fertility Trends', 6, 8, 9. T. H. C. Stevenson, 'The Fertility of Various Social Classes in England and Wales from the Middle of the Nineteenth Century to 1911', *Journal of the Royal Statistical Society*, 83 (1920), 431–2. M. R. Haines, 'Social Class Differentials During Fertility Decline: England and Wales Revisited', *Population Studies*, 43, 2 (1989), 307, 309, 315, 321. M. R. Haines, 'Occupation and Social Class during Fertility Decline: Historical Perspectives', in Gillis et al. (eds), *The European Experience*, pp. 196–202. R. I. Woods, 'Approaches to the Fertility Transition in Victorian England', *Population Studies*, 41, 2 (1987), 283–311.

62. J. A. and O. Banks, 'The Bradlaugh–Besant Trial and the English Newspapers', *Population Studies*, 8, 1 (1954), 22–34. Gittins, 'Married Life', 57–8. J. Lewis, 'The Ideology and Politics of Birth Control in Inter-war England', *Women's Studies International Quarterly*, 2 (1979), 33. J. Cleland and C. Wilson, 'Economic Theories of the Fertility Transition: an Iconoclastic View', *Population Studies*, 41, 1 (1987), 29. Woods, 'Approaches', 295–311.

63. As late as 1970 a quarter of all birth control practitioners in England and Wales still relied on the traditional withdrawal method. Van de Kaa, 'Recent Trends', 71.

64. N. F. R. Crafts, 'A Cross-Sectional Study of Legitimate Fertility in England and Wales, 1911', *Research in Economic History*, 9 (1984), 95, 105. N. F. R. Crafts, 'A Time Series Study of Fertility in England and Wales, 1877–1938', *European Journal of Economic History*, 13 (1984), 588–9. N. F. R. Crafts, 'Duration of Marriage, Fertility and Women's Employment Opportunities in England and Wales in 1911', *Population Studies*, 43, 2 (1989), 335. See also G. S. Becker, 'An Economic Analysis of Fertility', in National Bureau of Economic Research', *Demographic and Economic Change in Developed Countries* (Princeton, NJ, 1960) 227, 230. D. M. Heer, 'Economic Development and Fertility',

Demography, 3 (1966), 428. H. Liebenstein, 'An Interpretation of the Economic Theory of Fertility: Promising Path or Blind Alley?', *Journal of Economic Literature*, XII, 2 (1974), 459. Gittins, 'Married Life', 53–4. Woods, *The Population of Britain*, p. 49.

65. J. and P. Scheider, 'Going Forward in Reverse Gear: Culture, Economy and Political Economy in the Demographic Transition of a Rural Sicilian Town', in Gillis et al. (eds), *The European Experience*, pp. 146–74.

66. Chesnais, *The Demographic Transition*, p. 392.

67. Chesnais, *The Demographic Transition*, pp. 47, 138–51, 159, 332, 354, 513, 515–16. See also Teitelbaum, *The British Fertility Decline*, p. 222. D. Freidlander, 'Demographic Responses and Population Change', *Demography*, 6 (1969), 359–81.

68. Becker, 'An Economic Analysis', 227, 230. Friedlander, 'Demographic Responses', 360. Gittins, 'Married Life', 62. Cleland and Wilson, 'Economic Theories', 29. R. Freedman, 'The Sociology of Human Fertility: a Trend Report and Bibliography', *Current Sociology*, 10–11 (1961–2), 53–4. W. Seccombe, 'Men's "Marital Rights" and Women's "Wifely Duties": Changing Conjugal Relations in the Fertility Decline', in Gillis et al. (eds), *The European Experience*, p. 78.

69 Haines, 'Social Class', 307.

70. Crafts, 'A Cross-Sectional Study', 105. Crafts, 'A Time Series Study', 588.

71. Brass and Kabir, 'Regional Variations', 76, 78, 85. The failure of national average infant death rates in England and Wales to decline until after 1899/1900, a quarter of a century later than the onset of marital fertility decline, suggests that falling mortality made little or no contribution to the initiation of the fertility transition. For criticisms of the role of mortality see Woods, *The Population of Britain*, p. 50. Woods, 'Approaches', 293–5. Teitelbaum, *The British Fertility Decline*, p. 183. J. A. Banks, *Victorian Values. Secularism and the Size of Families* (London, 1981), pp. 122–3. Recent work by Lee, however, shows that in many parts of Britain a decline in infant death rates predated or accompanied the early decline in rates of marital fertility. Lee, 'Regional Inequalities', 55–65.

72. J. C. Simon, 'The Effect of Income on Fertility', *Population Studies*, 23, 3 (1969), 327–41. R. P. Beaujot, K. J. Krotki and P. Krishnan, 'Socio-Cultural Variations in the Applicability of the Economic Model of Fertility', *Population Studies*, 32, 2 (1978), 319–25.

73. Becker, 'An Economic Analysis', 227–8. J. Blake, 'Are Babies Consumer Durables?', *Population Studies*, 27, 1 (1968), 5–25.

Liebenstein, 'An Interpretation', 462–3, 465. Chesnais, *The Demographic Transition*, 356.

74. Heer, 'Economic Development', 427–8. D. M. Heer, 'Economic Development and the Fertility Transition', *Daedalus*, 97 (1968), 447–62.

75. Chesnais, *The Demographic Transition*, p. 356.

76. Crafts, 'A Cross-Sectional Study', 105. Anderson and Morse, 'High Fertility', 340. Gittins, 'Married Life', 58–61.

77. Liebenstein, 'An Interpretation', 459. A. T. Flegg, 'The Role of Inequality of Income in the Determination of Birth Rates', *Population Studies*, 33, 3 (1979), 457, 472. B. G. Zimmer, 'The Impact of Social Mobility on Fertility: a Reconsideration', *Population Studies*, 35, 1 (1981), 120, 122, 126, 130. M. S. L. Cook and R. Repetto, 'The Relevance of the Developing Countries to Demographic Transition Theory: Further Lessons from the Hungarian Experience', *Population Studies*, 36, 1 (1982), 111–28. A. K. Bhattacharyya, 'Income Inequality and Fertility: a Comparative View', *Population Studies*, 29, 1 (1975), 9. Gittins, *Fair Sex*, p. 182.

78. Haines, 'Fertility', 245–80. Gittins, *Fair Sex*, p. 185.

79. Gittins, 'Married Life', 55, 57, 61–3. Gittins, *Fair Sex*, p. 182. Crafts, 'Duration', 331, 335. Woods, *The Population of Britain*, pp. 50–1.

80. Simons, 'Developments', 125. N. Keyfitz, 'The Family That Does Not Reproduce Itself', in Davis et al. (eds), Below-Replacement, 140–1, 143–4, 148–9.

81. Freedman, 'The Sociology', 56.

82. Liebenstein, 'An Interpretation', 459. Keyfitz, 'The Family', 139–40, 146. Coleman and Salt, *The British Population*, pp. 64–5. L. H. Lees, 'Safety in Numbers: Social Welfare Legislation and Fertility Decline in Western Europe', in Davis et al. (eds), Below-Replacement, 310–25.

83. Liebenstein, 'An Interpretation', 459–60. Keyfitz, 'The Family', 141, 144, 146. Coleman and Salt, *The British Population*, pp. 64–5. Gittins, *Fair Sex*, p. 182. W. Minge-Kalman, 'The Industrial Revolution and the European Family: the Institutionalization of "Childhood" as a Market for Family Labour', *Comparative Studies in Society and History*, 20, 3 (1978), 454–68. J. C. Caldwell, 'The Mechanisms of Demographic Change in Historical Perspective', *Population Studies*, 35, 1 (1981), 9, 12, 19. D. Levine, 'Industrialization and the Proletarian Family in England', *Past and Present*, 107 (1985), 191–200. D. Levine, *Reproducing Families. The Political Economy*

of English Population History (Cambridge, 1987), pp. 162–214. According to Banks education contributes to the spread of family limitation in yet another way – through the effect of public examination systems in creating an historically unique state of mind in which individuals are encouraged to believe that equal efforts yield equal rewards. Banks, *Victorian Values*, pp. 132–7.

84. Keyfitz, 'The Family', 141, 144, 148.
85. Chesnais, *The Demographic Transition*, pp. 401–9.
86. R. V. Wells, 'Family History and the Demographic Transition', *Journal of Social History*, 9, 1 (1975), 6. Woods and Smith, 'The Decline', 208. Cleland and Wilson, 'Economic Theories', 25. Lesthaeghe, 'A Century', 413–14. Lesthaeghe and Meekers, 'Value changes', 225–7. Lesthaeghe and Surkyn, 'Cultural Dynamics', 2–3, 8.
87. Haines, 'Social Class', 322. Gittins, 'Married Life', 62–3. Seccombe, 'Men's "Marital Rights"', 66–84. J. R. Gillis, 'Gender and Fertility Decline Among the British Middle Classes', in Gillis et al. (eds), *The European Experience*, pp. 312–47. E. Ross, 'Mothers and the State in Britain, 1904–1914', in Gillis et al. (eds), *The European Experience*, pp. 48–65.
88. Wells, 'Family History', 6. Liebenstein, 'An Interpretation', 459. Lesthaeghe, 'A Century', 411–14, 429. Lesthaeghe and Surkyn, 'Cultural Dynamics', 4, 8, 15, 17. Cleland and Wilson, 'Economic Theories', 25, 28. Haines, 'Social Class', 306, 322. Coleman and Salt, *The British Population*, pp. 64, 66.
89. Chesnais, *The Demographic Transition*, p. 360. See also Liebenstein, 'An Interpretation', 470. Gittins, 'Married Life', 53. Gittins, *Fair Sex*, p. 187. Lesthaeghe, 'A Century', 411–15. Lesthaeghe and Meekers, 'Value Changes', 225–6. Lesthaeghe and Surkyn, 'Cultural Dynamics', 2, 8. Keyfitz, 'The Family', 139. Cleland and Wilson, 'Economic Theories', 5.
90. See, for example, Becker, 'An Economic Analysis', 210. Bhattacharyya, 'Income Inequality', 6. Crafts, 'Duration', 335. Anderson and Morse, 'High Fertility', 343.
91. For example, Cleland and Wilson, 'Economic Theories', 25, 27–8. Chesnais, *The Demographic Transition*, p. 360. Coleman and Salt, *The British Population*, p. 66. J. R. Gillis, L. A. Tilly and D. Levine, 'The Quiet Revolution', in Gillis et al. (eds), *The European Experience*, pp. 1–9.
92. Chesnais, *The Demographic Transition*, p. 392. Gillis et al., 'The Quiet Revolution', pp. 1–9. M. J. Maynes, 'The Contours of Childhood: Demography, Strategy and Mythology of Childhood

in French and German Lower Class Autobiographies', in Gillis et al. (eds), *The European Experience*, pp. 101–24.

93. Woods and Smith, 'The Decline', 207–9, 225. Chesnais, *The Demographic Transition*, pp. 409, 471. Coleman and Salt, *The British Population*, pp. 62–3. M. Segalen, 'Exploring a Cause of Late French Fertility Decline: Two Contrasted Breton Examples', in Gillis et al. (eds), *The European Experience*, pp. 227–47. Simon, 'The Effect', 331. Liebenstein, 'An Interpretation', 469–71. Teitelbaum, *The British Fertility Decline*, p. 218. Keyfitz, 'The Family', 141. G. B. Terry, 'Rival Explanations in the Work–Fertility Relationship', *Population Studies*, 29, 2 (1975), 191.

94. Simons, 'Developments', 117. Murphy, 'Economic Models', 235.

95. 'A Review of the 1980s', *Population Trends*, 62 (1990), 6. B. Botting, 'Trends in Abortion', *Population Trends*, 64 (1991), 19–20, 23, 26–7.

96. Coleman and Salt, *The British Population*, p. 126. See also Leshaeghe, 'A Century', 412. S. H. Preston, 'Changing Values and Falling Birth Rates', in Davis et al. (eds), Below-Replacement, 187. Of all industrialised countries only in Japan has abortion played a particularly important role in the further decline in fertility in recent decades. Preston, 'The Decline', 42.

97. Botting, 'Trends', 24–5. M. Murphy, 'The Contraceptive Pill and Women's Employment as Factors in Fertility Change in Britain, 1963–1980: a Challenge to the Conventional View', *Population Studies*, 47, 2 (1993), 227–8.

98. Simons, 'Developments', 127, 130. Ermisch, 'The Relevance', 42, 53. Coleman and Salt, *The British Population*, p. 123

99. Preston, 'Changing Values', 182–4.

100. Ni Bhrolchain, 'Period Parity', 122.

101. Murphy, 'The Contraceptive Pill', 221, 223–4, 229, 236–8. See also Murphy, 'Economic Models', 241–2.

102. E. de Cooman, J. Ermisch and H. Joshi, 'The Next Birth and the Labour Market: a Dynamic Model of Births in England and Wales', *IPPF Medical Bulletin*, 16/4 (1982), 2–4. Ermisch, 'Investigations', 141, 152. Lesthaeghe and Meekers, 'Value Changes', 231. Lesthaeghe and Surkyn, 'Cultural Dynamics', 32, 34. Coleman and Salt, *The British Population*, pp. 122–3, 126. Murphy, 'Economic Models', 250.

103. Glass, 'Fertility Trends', 103. Gittins, 'Married Life', 60–1. Simons, 'Developments', 123. Coleman and Salt, *The British Population*, pp. 115, 138. Winter, 'War, Family and Fertility', 292.

104. Coleman and Salt, *The British Population*, pp. 117, 143. Ermisch, 'The Relevance', 50, 53. Ermisch, 'Investigations', 146, 153. M. Ni Bhrolchain, 'The Interpretation and Role of Work-Associated Accelerated Childbearing in Postwar Britain', *European Journal of Population*, 2 (1986), 135–54. M. Ni Bhrolchain, 'Women's Paid Work and Timing of Births: Longitudinal Evidence', *European Journal of Population*, 2 (1986), 43–70. De Cooman et al., 'The Next Birth', 255. Winter, 'War, Family and Fertility', 292–3. Busfield and Hawthorn, 'Some Social Determinants', 65, 74. Data from the 1976 OPCS Family Formation Survey suggest that housing conditions were the single most important influence on social class fertility differentials. N. J. Murphy, 'Differential Family Formation in Great Britain', *Journal of Biosocial Science*, 19 (1987), 482. The nature of housing tenure also helped shape regional fertility variations in England and Wales. Coward, 'Fertility Patterns', 84.

105. Ermisch, 'Investigations', 154–5. De Cooman et al., 'The Next Birth', 261–3. Coleman and Salt, *The British Population*, pp. 138–9. Preston, 'Changing Values', 179, 184.

106. Ermisch, 'Investigations', 153. Murphy, however, argues that, because owner-occupiers have lower fertility than those who rent, part of the explanation for declining rates of fertility after the mid 1960s was the increase which occurred in the percentage of young couples owning their own houses. M. J. Murphy, 'Housing the People: From Shortage to Surplus', in Joshi (ed.), *The Changing Population*, pp. 100–1.

107. R. A. Easterlin, 'The American Baby Boom in Historical Perspective', *American Economic Review*, 51 (1961), 869–911. R. A. Easterlin, 'The Conflict between Aspirations and Resources', *Population and Development Review*, 2, 3 & 4 (1976), 417–25.

108. V. K. Oppenheimer, 'The Easterlin Hypothesis: Another Aspect of the Echo to Consider', *Population and Development Review*, 2 (1976), 433–58.

109. J. F. Ermisch, 'Time Costs Aspirations and the Effect of Economic Growth on German Fertility', *Oxford Bulletin of Economics and Statistics*, 42, 2 (1980), 125–43. Ermisch, 'Investigations', 144. Socio-occupational differentials in fertility in the USA between 1930 and 1960 likewise fail to conform to the Easterlin thesis. A. Sweezy, 'The Economic Explanation of Fertility Changes in the United States', *Population Studies*, 25, 2 (1971), 260–2.

110. Crafts, 'A Time Series Study', 584, 589.

111. Ermisch, 'The Relevance', 40, 45–8. Ermisch, 'Investigations', 143–4.
112. Ermisch, 'The Relevance', 47–9.
113. Robert E. Wright, 'The Easterlin Hypothesis and European Fertility Rates', *Population and Development Review*, 15, 1 (1989), 109, 117–18.
114. Coleman and Salt, *The British Population*, p. 140.
115. R. J. Willis, 'A New Approach to the Economic Theory of Fertility Behaviour', *Journal of Political Economy*, 81, 2, Part II (1973), 514–64. W. P. Butz and M. P. Ward, 'Will US Fertility Remain Low? A New Economic Interpretation', *Population and Development Review*, 5, 4 (1979), 663–89. Ermisch, 'The Relevance', 40–2, 50. Ermisch, 'Investigations', 144–6. Even Lesthaeghe, the main protagonist of ideationalist interpretations, accepts that increases in female employment made some contribution to the decline in fertility from the mid 1960s. Lesthaeghe, 'A Century', 415–16. Lesthaeghe and Meekers, 'Value Changes', 261.
116. H. Joshi, 'The Changing Form of Women's Employment Dependency', in Joshi (ed.), *The Changing Population*, p. 158.
117. Similar increases occurred in almost all industrialised countries. Ermisch, 'The Labour Market', 179–81. Coleman and Salt, *The British Population*, p. 141.
118. H. Joshi, 'The Cash Opportunity Costs of Childbearing: an Approach to Estimation Using British Data', *Population Studies*, 44, 1 (1990), 53.
119. Ermisch, 'The Relevance', 52. Ermisch, 'Investigations', 149. De Cooman et al., 'The Next Birth', 255–7. Wright, 'The Easterlin Hypothesis', 118–19.
120. De Cooman et al., 'The Next Birth', 260. For similar conclusions on the importance of increasing female employment for Scottish fertility rates since 1964 see Kendrick et al., 'Recent Trends', 44–5.
121. Ermisch, 'Investigations', 155.
122. H. Jones, 'A Spatial Analysis of Human Fertility in Scotland', *Scottish Geographic Magazine*, 91 (1975), 102–13. M. Wilson, 'A Spatial Analysis of Human Fertility in Scotland: Reappraisal and Extension', *Scottish Geographic Magazine*, 94 (1978), 130–43. Coward, 'Fertility Patterns', 18–19. Kendrick et al., 'Recent Trends', 44–5, 47. Murphy, 'Differential Family Formation', 463–4.
123. Preston, 'The Decline of Fertility', 26, 28.
124. Murphy, 'Economic Models', 243.
125. Ni Bhrolchain, 'Period Parity', 123.

126. Murphy, 'Economic Models', 250.
127. Simons, 'Developments', 131, 133–4. Lesthaeghe, 'A Century', 430. Lesthaeghe and Meekers, 'Value Changes', 226, 261. Lesthaeghe and Surkyn, 'Cultural Dynamics', 32–6. Preston, 'Changing Values', 180–1, 189. Coleman and Salt, *The British Population*, pp. 146–7. Murphy, 'Economic Models', 241. Winter, 'War, Family and Fertility', 293, 305–8.
128. Murphy, 'Economic Models', 250.

BIBLIOGRAPHY

This is a highly selective list of books and articles intended as a guide to further reading.

Books

Baines, D., *Migration in a Mature Economy. Emigration and Internal Migration in England and Wales, 1861–1900* (Cambridge, 1985).

Baines, D., *Emigration from Europe, 1815–1930* (London, 1991).

Barker, T. and Drake, M. (eds), *Population and Society in Britain, 1850–1980* (London, 1982).

Champion, A. G. (ed.), *Counterurbanization. The Changing Pace and Nature of Population Deconcentration* (London, 1989).

Chesnais, J.-C., *The Demographic Transition. Stages, Patterns and Economic Implications* (Oxford, 1992).

Coleman, D. A. (ed.), *Demography of Immigrants and Minority Groups in the United Kingdom* (London, 1982).

Coleman, D. and Salt, J., *The British Population. Patterns, Trends and Processes* (Oxford, 1992).

Davis, K., Bernstam, M. S. and Ricardo-Campbell, R. (eds), 'Below-Replacement, Fertility in Industrial Societies. Causes, Consequences, Policies', *Population and Development Review*, Supplement to vol. 12 (1986).

Eversely, D. and Kolmann, W. (eds), *Population Changes and Social Planning* (London, 1982).

Flinn, M. W. (ed.), *Scottish Population History from the Seventeenth Century to the 1930s* (Cambridge, 1977).

Gillis, J. R., Tilly, L. A. and Levine, D. (eds), *The European Experience of Declining Fertility. A Quiet Revolution, 1850–1970* (Oxford, 1992).

Gittins, D., *Fair Sex, Family Size and Structure, 1900–39* (London, 1982).

Goddard, J. B. and Champion A. G. (eds), *The Urban and Regional Transformation of Britain* (London, 1983).

Hiorns, R. W. (ed.), *Demographic Patterns in Developed Societies* (London, 1980).

Hobcraft, J. and Rees, P. (eds), *Regional Demographic Development* (London, 1978).

Jones, H. (ed.), *Population Change in Contemporary Scotland* (Norwich, 1984).

Joshi, H. (ed.), *The Changing Population of Britain* (Oxford, 1990).

Levine, D., *Reproducing Families. The Political Economy of English Population History* (Cambridge, 1987).

Livi-Bacci, M., *A Concise History of World Population* (Oxford, 1992).

McKeown, T., *The Modern Rise of Population* (London, 1976).

Mercer, A. J., *Disease, Mortality and Population in Transition. Epidemiological-Demographic Change in England since the Eighteenth Century as Part of a Global Phenomenon* (Leicester, 1990).

Pacione, M. (ed.) *Population Geography: Progress and Prospect* (London, 1986).

Shorter, E., *The Making of the Modern Family* (London, 1977).

Teitelbaum, M. S., *The British Fertility Decline* (Princeton, 1984).

Walvin, J., *Passage to Britain. Immigration in British History and Politics* (Hardmondsworth, 1984).

White, P. E and Van Der Knaap, Bert. (eds), *Contemporary Studies of Migration* (Norwich, 1985).

Woods, R., *The Population of Britain in the Nineteenth Century* (London, 1992).

Woods, R. and Rees, P. (eds), *Population Structures and Models. Development in Spatial Demography* (London, 1986).

Articles

Anderson, M. and Morse, D. J., 'High Fertility, High Emigration, Low Nuptiality: Adjustment Processes in Scotland's Demographic

Experience, 1861–1914, Part II', *Population Studies*, 47, 2 (1993), 319–43.

Becker, G. S., 'An Economic Analysis of Fertility', in National Bureau of Economic Research', *Demographic and Economic Change in Developed Countries* (Princeton, NJ, 1960), pp. 423–44.

Beaver, M. W., 'Population, Infant Mortality and Milk', *Population Studies*, 27, 2 (1973), 243–54.

Blake, J., 'Are Babies Consumer Durables?' *Population Studies*, 22, 1 (1968), 5–25.

Busfield, J. and Hawthorn, G., 'Some Social Determinants of Recent Trends in British Fertility', *Journal of Biosocial Science*, Sup. 3 (1971), 65–77.

Butz, W. P. and Ward, M. P., 'Will US Fertility Remain Low? A New Economic Interpretation', *Population and Development Review*, 5, 4 (1989), 663–89.

Caldwell, J. C., 'The Mechanisms of Demographic Change in Historical Perspective', *Population Studies*, 35, 1 (1981), 5–27.

Calot, G. and Blayo, C., 'Recent Course of Fertility in Western Europe', *Population Studies*, 36, 3 (1982), 349–72.

Cleland, J. and Wilson, C., 'Demand Theories of the Fertility Transition: An Iconoclastic View', *Population Studies*, 41, 1 (1987), 5–30.

Cooper, J., 'Births Outside Marriage: Recent Trends and Associated Demographic and Social Changes', *Population Trends*, 63 (1991), 8–18.

Crafts, N. F. R., 'Illegitimacy in England and Wales in 1911', *Population Studies*, 36, 2 (1982), 327–31.

Crafts, N. F. R., 'A Cross-Sectional Study of Legitimate Fertility in England and Wales, 1911', *Research in Economic History*, 9 (1984), 89–107.

Crafts, N. F. R., 'A Time Series Study of Fertility in England and Wales, 1877–1938', *Journal of European Economic History*, 13 (1984), 571–90.

Crafts, N. F. R., 'Duration of Marriage, Fertility and Women's Employment Opportunities in England and Wales in 1911', *Population Studies*, 43, 2 (1989), 325–35.

De Cooman, E., Ermisch, J. and Joshi, H., 'The Next Birth and the Labour Market: a Dynamic Model of Births in England and Wales', *Population Studies*, 41, 2 (1987), 237–68.

Dyhouse, C., 'Working Class Mothers and Infant Mortality in England, 1895–1914', *Journal of Social History*, 12, 2 (1978), 248–67.

Easterlin, R. A., 'The American Baby Boom in Historical Perspective', *American Economic Review*, 51 (1961), 869–911.

Easterlin, R. A., 'The Conflict between Aspirations and Resources', *Population and Development Review*, 2 (1976), 417–26.

Eldridge, S. and Kiernan, K., 'Declining First-Marriage Rates in England and Wales: a Change in Timing or a Rejection of Marriage?', *European Journal of Population*, 1 (1985), 327–45.

Ermisch, J. F., 'The Relevance of the Easterlin Hypothesis and the "New Home Economics" to Fertility Movement in Great Britain', *Population Studies*, 33, 1 (1979), 39–58.

Fielding, A. J., 'Counterurbanization in Western Europe', *Progress in Planning*, 17, 1 (1982), 5–34.

Fox, E., 'Powers of Life and Death: Aspects of Maternal Welfare in England and Wales between the Wars', *Medical History*, 35 (1991), 328–52.

Freedman, R., 'The Sociology of Human Fertility: a Trend Report and Bibliography', *Current Sociology*, 10–11 (1961–2), 35–68.

Friedlander, D., 'The Spread of Urbanization in England and Wales, 1851–1951', *Population Studies*, 24, 3 (1970), 423–43.

Friedlander, D. and Roshier, R. J., 'A Study of Internal Migration in England and Wales, Part II', *Population Studies*, 19, 3 (1966), 45–59.

Gage, T. B., 'The Decline of Mortality in England and Wales, 1861 to 1964: Decomposition by Cause of Death and Component of Mortality', *Population Studies*, 47, 1 (1953), 47–66.

Gittins, D., 'Married Life and Birth Control between the Wars', *Oral History*, III, 2 (1975), 52–64.

Glass, D. V., 'Fertility Trends in Europe since the Second World War', *Population Studies*, 22, 1 (1968), 103–46.

Gould, J. D., 'European Inter-Continental Emigration, 1815–1914: Patterns and Causes', *Journal of European Economic History*, 8, 3 (1979), 593–680.

Gould, J. D., 'European Inter-Continental Emigration the Road Home: Return Migration from the USA', *Journal of European Economic History*, 9, 1 (1980), 41–112.

Gould, J. D., 'European Inter-Continental Emigration: the Role of Diffusion and Feedback', *Journal of European Economic History*, 9, 2 (1980), 267–315.

Haines, M. R., 'Social Class Differentials During Fertility Decline: England and Wales Revisited', *Population Studies*, 43, 2 (1989), 305–22.

Hajnal, J., 'Age at Marriage and Proportions Marrying', *Population Studies*, 7, 2 (1953), 111–36.

Heer, D. M., 'Economic Development and Fertility', *Demography*, 3 (1966), 423–44.

Heer, D. M., 'Economic Development and the Fertility Transition', *Daedalus*, 97 (1968), 447–62.

Laslett, P. and Oosterveen, K., 'Long-Term Trends in Bastardy in England: a Study of Illegitimacy Figures in the Parish Registers and in the Reports of the Registrar-General, 1561–1960', *Population Studies*, 27, 2 (1973), 255–86.

Law, C. M., 'The Growth of Urban Population in England and Wales, 1801–1911', *Transactions of the Institute of British Geographers*, XLI (1967), 125–43.

Lee, C. H., 'Regional Inequalities in Infant Mortality in Britain, 1861–1971: Patterns and Hypotheses', *Population Studies*, 45, 1 (1991), 55–65.

Lesthaeghe, R., 'A Century of Demographic and Cultural Change in Western Europe: an Explanation of Underlying Dimensions', *Population and Development Review*, 9, 3 (1983), 411–35.

Lesthaeghe, R. and Meekers, D., 'Value Changes and the Dimensions of Familism in the European Community', *European Journal of Population*, 2 (1986), 225–68.

Lesthaeghe, R. and Surkyn, J., 'Cultural Dynamics and Economic Theories of Fertility Change', *Population and Development Review*, 14 (1988), 1–45.

Levine, D., 'Industrialization and the Proletarian Family in England', *Past and Present*, 107 (1985), 168–203.

Lewis, J., 'The Ideology and Politics of Birth Control in Inter-War England', *Women's Studies International Quarterly*, 2 (1979), 33–48.

Liebenstein, H., 'An Interpretation of the Economic Theory of Fertility: Promising Path or Blind Alley?' *Journal of Economic Literature*, XII, 2 (1974), 457–79.

Logan, W. P. D., 'Mortality in England and Wales from 1848 to 1947', *Population Studies*, 4, 2 (1950), 132–78.

Loudon, I., 'Maternal Mortality: 1880–1950. Some Regional and International Comparisons', *Society for the Social History of Medicine*, 1 (1988), 183–228.

Loudon, I., 'On Maternal and Infant Mortality, 1900–1960', *Society for the Social History of Medicine*, 4 (1991), 29–73.

Marr, W. L. 'The United Kingdom's Inter-Continental Migration in the Inter-War Period: Theoretical Considerations and Empirical Testing', *Population Studies*, 31, 3 (1977), 571–9.

Massey, D. S., 'Economic Development and International Migration in Comparative Perspective', *Population and Development Review*, 14, 3 (1988), 383–413.

McAvinchey, I. D., 'Economic Factors and Mortality. Some Aspects of the Scottish Case, 1950–78', *Scottish Journal of Political Economy*, 31, 1 (1984), 1–27.

McKeown, T., Brown, R. G. and Record, R. G., 'An Interpretation of the Modern Rise of Population in Europe', *Population Studies*, 26, 3 (1972), 345–82.

McKeown, T., Record, R. G. and Turner, R. D., 'An Interpretation of the Decline in Mortality in England and Wales during the 20th Century', *Population Studies*, 29, 3 (1975), 391–422.

Mercer, A. J., 'Relative Trends in Mortality from Related Respiratory and Airborne Infectious Diseases', *Population Studies*, 40, 1 (1986), 129–45.

Minge-Kalman, W., 'The Industrial Revolution and the European Family: the Institutionalization of "Childhood" as a Market for Family Labour', *Comparative Studies in Society and History*, 20, 3 (1975), 454–68.

Murphy, M., 'Economic Models of Fertility in Post-War Britain – a Conceptual and Statistical Reinterpretation', *Population Studies*, 46, 2 (1992), 235–58.

Murphy, M., 'The Contraceptive Pill and Women's Employment as Factors in Fertility Change in Britain, 1963–1980: a Challenge to the Conventional View', *Population Studies*, 47, 2 (1993), 221–43.

Ni Bhrolchain, M., 'The Interpretation and Role of Work-Associated Accelerated Childbearing in Postwar Britain', *European Journal of Population*, 2 (1986), 135–54.

Ni Bhrolchain, M., 'Women's Paid Work and the Timing of Births: Longitudinal Evidence', *European Journal of Population*, 2 (1986), 43–70.

Oppenheimer, V. K., 'The Easterlin Hypothesis: Another Aspect of the Echo to Consider', *Population and Development Review*, 2 (1976), 433–58.

Pamuk, E. R., 'Social Class Inequality in Mortality from 1921 to 1972 in England and Wales', *Population Studies*, 39, 1 (1985), 15–31.

Pope, D., 'Some Factors Inhibiting Australian Immigration in the 1920s', *Australian Economic History Review*, 24, 1 (1984), 34–52.

Schoen, R. and Baj, J., 'Twentieth Century Cohort Marriage and Divorce in England and Wales', *Population Studies*, 38, 3 (1984), 439–49.

Shorter, E., 'Female Emancipation, Birth Control and Fertility in European History', *American Historical Review*, 78, 3 (1973), 605–40.

Shorter, E., Knodel, J. and Van De Walle, E., 'The Decline of Non-Marital Fertility in Europe, 1880–1940', *Population Studies*, 25, 3 (1971), 375–93.

Simon, J. C., 'The Effect of Income on Fertility', *Population Studies*, 23, 3 (1969), 327–41.

Terry, G. B., 'Rival Explanations in the Work–Fertility Relationship', *Population Studies*, 29, 2 (1975), 191–205.

Tilly, L. A., Scott, J. W. and Cohen, M., 'Women's Work and European Fertility Patterns', *Journal of Interdisciplinary History*, VI, 3 (1976), 447–76.

Watkins, S. C., 'Regional Patterns of Nuptiality in Europe, 1870–1960', *Population Studies*, 35, 2 (1981), 199–215.

Watkins, S. C., 'From Local to National Communities: the Transformation of Demographic Regimes in Western Europe, 1870–1960', *Population and Development Review*, 16, 2 (1990), 241–72.

Watterson, P. A., 'Role of the Environment in the Decline of Infant Mortality: an Analysis of the 1911 Census of England and Wales', *Journal of Biosocial Science*, 18 (1986), 457–70.

Watterson, P. A., 'Infant Mortality Decline by Father's Occupation from the 1911 Census of England and Wales', *Demography*, 25, 2 (1988), 289–305.

Wells, R. V., 'Family History and the Demographic Transition', *Journal of Social History*, 9, 1 (1975), 1–19.

Willis, R. J., 'A New Approach to the Economic Theory of Fertility', *Journal of Political Economy*, 81, 2, Part II (1973), 514–64.

Wilson, C. and Woods, R. I., 'Fertility in England: a Long-Term Perspective', *Population Studies*, 45, 3 (1991), 399–415.

Winter, J. M., 'Aspects of the Impact of the First World War on Infant Mortality in Britain', *Journal of European Economic History*, 11, 3 (1972), 713–18.

Winter, J. M., 'Some Aspects of the Demographic Consequences of the First World War in Britain', *Population Studies*, 30, 3 (1976), 539–52.

Winter, J. M., 'The Impact of the First World War on Civilian Health in Britain', *Economic History Review*, 30, 3 (1977), 487–507.

Winter, J. M., 'Infant Mortality, Maternal Mortality and Public Health in Britain', *Journal of European Economic History*, 13, 2 (1979), 439–62.

Woods, R. I., 'Approaches to the Fertility Transition in Victorian England', *Population Studies*, 41, 2 (1987), 283–311.

Woods, R. I., Watterson, P. A. and Woodward, J. H., 'The Causes of Rapid Infant Mortality Decline in England and Wales, 1861–1921. Part I', *Population Studies*, 42, 3 (1988), 343–66.

Woods, R. I., Watterson, P. A. and Woodward J. H., 'The Causes of Rapid Infant Mortality Decline in England and Wales, 1861–1921. Part II', *Population Studies*, 43, 1 (1989), 113–32.

Wright, Robert E., 'The Easterlin Hypothesis and European Fertility Rates', *Population and Development Review*, 15, 1 (1989), 107–22.

INDEX